REPENTANCE AND FORGIVENESS

The Pro Ecclesia Series

Books in The Pro Ecclesia Series are "for the church." The series is sponsored by the Center for Catholic and Evangelical Theology, founded by Carl Braaten and Robert Jenson in 1991. The series seeks to nourish the church's faithfulness to the gospel of Jesus Christ through a theology that is self-critically committed to the biblical, dogmatic, liturgical, and ethical traditions that form the foundation for a fruitful ecumenical theology. The series reflects a commitment to the classical tradition of the church as providing the resources critically needed by the various churches as they face modern and post-modern challenges. The series will include books by individuals as well as collections of essays by individuals and groups. The Editorial Board will be drawn from various Christian traditions.

TITLES IN THE SERIES INCLUDE:

The Morally Divided Body: Ethical Disagreement and the Unity of the Church, edited by Michael Root and James J. Buckley

Christian Theology and Islam, edited by Michael Root and James J. Buckley

Who Do You Say That I Am?: Proclaiming and Following Jesus Today, edited by Michael Root and James J. Buckley

What Does It Mean to "Do This"?: Supper, Mass, Eucharist, edited by Michael Root and James J. Buckley

Heaven, Hell, . . . and Purgatory?, edited by Michael Root and James J. Buckley

Life Amid the Principalities: Identifying, Understanding, and Engaging Created, Fallen, and Disarmed Powers Today, edited by Michael Root and James J. Buckley

Remembering the Reformation: Commemorate? Celebrate? Repent?, edited by Michael Root and James J. Buckley

The Emerging Christian Minority, edited by Victor Lee Austin and Joel C. Daniels

What's the Good of Humanity?, edited by Victor Lee Austin and Joel C. Daniels

Repentance and Forgiveness

Edited by
Matthew E. Burdette and
Victor Lee Austin

CASCADE *Books* • Eugene, Oregon

REPENTANCE AND FORGIVENESS

Pro Ecclesia Series 9

Copyright © 2020 Wipf and Stock Publishers. All rights reserved. Except for brief quotations in critical publications or reviews, no part of this book may be reproduced in any manner without prior written permission from the publisher. Write: Permissions, Wipf and Stock Publishers, 199 W. 8th Ave., Suite 3, Eugene, OR 97401.

Cascade Books
An Imprint of Wipf and Stock Publishers
199 W. 8th Ave., Suite 3
Eugene, OR 97401

www.wipfandstock.com

PAPERBACK ISBN: 978-1-5326-6043-6
HARDCOVER ISBN: 978-1-5326-6044-3
EBOOK ISBN: 978-1-5326-6045-0

Cataloguing-in-Publication data:

Names: Burdette, Matthew E., editor. | Austin, Victor Lee, editor.

Title: Repentance and forgiveness / edited by Matthew E. Burdette and Victor Lee Austin.

Description: Eugene, OR : Cascade Books, 2020 | Pro Ecclesia Series 9 | Includes bibliographical references.

Identifiers: ISBN 978-1-5326-6043-6 (paperback) | ISBN 978-1-5326-6044-3 (hardcover) | ISBN 978-1-5326-6045-0 (ebook)

Subjects: LCSH: Repentance | Forgiveness.

Classification: BJ1476 .R46 2020 (print) | BJ1476 .R46 (ebook)

Manufactured in the U.S.A.   JUNE 4, 2020

Revised Standard Version of the Bible, copyright © 1946, 1952, and 1971 the Division of Christian Education of the National Council of the Churches of Christ in the United States of America. Used by permission. All rights reserved.

New Revised Standard Version Bible, copyright 1989, Division of Christian Education of the National Council of the Churches of Christ in the United States of America. Used by permission. All rights reserved.

Contents

List of Contributors vii

Preface x
    Matthew E. Burdette and Victor Lee Austin

1 Repentance and Forgiveness: Biblical Foundations 1
   Stephen Westerholm

2 A Psycho-theological Reading of Repentance and Forgiveness in Judaism and Christianity 21
   Ellen T. Charry

3 The Virtue of the Sacrament of Penance:
   A Thomist Reply to Lutheran Concerns 36
   Dominic M. Langevin, OP

4 Is Reconciliation Still Relevant? Reflections on a Theological Theme in an Era of Diversity and Inclusivity 62
   John P. Burgess

5 "I Am the Foremost of Sinners" (1 Tim 1:15): Negotiating the Church's Language of Self-Condemnation 73
   Peter C. Bouteneff

6 Confession and Repentance in the Emerging Technoculture 84
   Brent Waters

Contributors

Victor Lee Austin is the Theologian-in-Residence for the Episcopal Diocese of Dallas and is the author of several books including *Losing Susan: Brain Disease, the Priest's Wife, and the God Who Gives and Takes Away*.

Peter C. Bouteneff teaches courses in ancient and modern theology and spirituality at St. Vladimir's Orthodox Seminary, where he is Professor of Systematic Theology. He has worked for many years in theological dialogue, notably as Executive Secretary for Faith and Order at the World Council of Churches, and has written extensively on Orthodox relations with other churches. He conceived of and edits the Foundations series for St. Vladimir's Seminary Press, to which he has contributed a volume called *Sweeter than Honey: Orthodox Thinking on Dogma and Truth* (2006). In 2008 he authored a study of how early Christians read the Genesis creation accounts, called *Beginnings: Ancient Christian Readings of the Biblical Creation Narratives*. As director of the seminary's Sacred Arts Initiative, and its Arvo Pärt Project, he authored *Arvo Pärt: Out of Silence*, exploring the connections between the great Estonian composer's music and his faith. He most recent book is *How to Be a Sinner: Finding Yourself in the Language of Repentance*, which explores more thoroughly some of the themes explored in his chapter in the present volume.

Matthew E. Burdette is rector of Saint Christopher's Episcopal Church in Dallas and holds a PhD in theology from the University of Aberdeen, having researched the theology of Robert W. Jenson and James H. Cone.

John P. Burgess is the James Henry Snowden Professor of Systematic Theology at Pittsburgh Theological Seminary. He has spoken and published widely on theology for the church. His most recent book is *Holy Rus': The Rebirth of Orthodoxy in the New Russia* (2017). He is an ordained minister in the Presbyterian Church (USA).

Contributors

Ellen T. Charry is the Margaret W. Harmon Professor of Theology Emerita of Princeton Theological Seminary. Her works include *Psalms 1–50: Sighs and Songs of Israel* (2015); *The Austin Dogmatics of Paul M. van Buren*, ed. (2012); *God and the Art of Happiness* (2010); *Inquiring after God*, ed. (2000); *By the Renewing of Your Minds* (1997); and *Franz Rosenzweig on the Freedom of God* (1987). Her work in progress is "The Wall of Hostility Has Come Down: Rethinking the Relationship between Judaism and Christianity."

Dominic M. Langevin, OP, is Assistant Professor of Systematic Theology at the Pontifical Faculty of the Immaculate Conception at the Dominican House of Studies, Washington, DC. He has previously studied at Yale University (BA), his current faculty (MDiv, STB, STL), and the University of Fribourg, Switzerland (STD). He is the author of *From Passion to Paschal Mystery* (2015). He is the editor of the journal *The Thomist*. His primary research interest is sacramental theology.

Brent Waters is the Jerre and Mary Joy Stead Professor of Christian Social Ethics, and Director of the Jerre L. and Mary Joy Stead Center for Ethics and Values at Garrett-Evangelical Theological Seminary. He is the author of several books, including *Just Capitalism: A Christian Ethic of Globalization*; *Christian Moral Theology in the Emerging Technoculture: From Posthuman Back to Human*; *This Mortal Flesh: Incarnation and Bioethics*; *The Family in Christian Social and Political Thought*; and *From Human to Posthuman: Christian Theology and Technology in a Postmodern World*.

Stephen Westerholm is Professor Emeritus of Early Christianity, Department of Religious Studies, McMaster University, where he taught from 1984 to 2017.

Preface

SIN IS ESSENTIALLY THE creation of distance and disunity where there had been closeness and unity. It is the fracturing of relationships. In the catechism of our denomination, there is an implicit assumption that the human being has four fundamental relationships: with God, with other people, with the created world, and with herself (if in fact it makes any sense to speak of a relationship with yourself). All those relationships are broken to some degree by sin. We are out of harmony with God, and, consequently, with other people, and with the world at large. And we are fractured within ourselves, the principal sign of which, arguably, is our divided will. "Wretched man that I am!" exclaimed the Apostle, contemplating his failure to do what he wanted to do and his doing that which he did not want to do. Or one thinks of Augustine beseeching the Lord to unite his fractured self, to give him a whole will, and thus, in particular, to give him chastity ... but not yet!

To restore closeness and unity, to bring reconciliation, is the heart of Christianity. It is the cosmic business of the incarnation, the cross, and the exaltation of Christ: that all people be drawn to God, and that it be possible for all people to be drawn to God, and thus for the brokenness in all its dimensions to be overcome. But to be reconciled is not a matter of the snapping of the divine fingers. It is not, for us as doers or as thinkers, a simple matter. It is in fact a call, a summons to repent and to be forgiven, and then, concomitantly, to forgive. And that is one reason why, instead of calling the conference where these essays originated one on, simply, "Reconciliation," we were more specific and called it "Repentance and Forgiveness."

We gathered to reexamine these fundamental Christian claims, so easily stated, so easily relegated to the background noise of our lives, so easily ignored, and yet so difficultly plumbed. It is a good thing, a sort of public witness, for Christians to come together around a subject that, one would think, is so obvious. This volume says, in effect, that Christians need,

Preface

today as perhaps always, to return to their roots, to put their hands again on the heart of Christ, repentance and forgiveness.

Matthew E. Burdette
Victor Lee Austin

1

Repentance and Forgiveness: Biblical Foundations

Stephen Westerholm

"Repentance and forgiveness in the Bible" is a huge topic, far beyond anything that can be covered in one paper; so let's begin by making the topic even bigger. I want to begin with a brief look at the general framework within Scripture for its summons to repentance, then look at some implications of that framework for our topic. After that I want us to think briefly about a curious question indirectly but importantly related to our topic: Does God repent? Then we'll get to the nitty-gritty: specific texts, first in the Old Testament, then in the New, in which our theme plays a significant role.

The Framework of Scripture's Summons to Repentance

Before we begin our look at repentance and forgiveness in Scripture, something should be said about the *framework* within which the summons to repentance has its necessary place. I hope not to labor the obvious; I do want to make sure that the obvious is not overlooked. Before the cosmos came into being, before (if you will allow the expression) time itself had begun, there was God: "Before the mountains were brought forth, or ever thou hadst formed the earth and the world, from everlasting to everlasting thou art God" (Ps 90:2).[1] But "in the beginning" of time as we know it, "God created the heavens and the earth" (Gen 1:1). And "God created humankind in his image" (Gen 1:27, NRSV) to exercise dominion over the earth (Gen 1:28; cf. Ps 115:16) and to enjoy both *its* goodness and fellowship with its Creator (Gen 2:9, 16; 3:8), while acknowledging, through obedience to a single command, their place as created beings and mere *recipients* of all that is good (Gen 2:17). That, sufficiently for our purposes, takes us through Genesis 1 and 2.

So we are only as far as chapter 3 of the Bible's 1189 chapters (or, if you prefer, 1334 chapters) when all this is spoiled; and the story of the rest of the Bible is about how God puts things right again. It is *not* right that human beings—made by God in God's image, their every breath and heartbeat dependent upon God, their every good a gift from God—should refuse to acknowledge God or render God due honor and thanks. This fundamental sin, this capital *S* "Sin," lies at the root of all particular sins, all small *s* "sins," since those who refuse to acknowledge their Creator go on to express that refusal by transgressing the created order as well. Paul spells out the process in the first chapter of Romans. "Although [people] knew God they did not honor him as God or give thanks to him. . . . Therefore God gave them up" to sins against nature itself. "And since they did not see fit to acknowledge God, God gave them up to a base mind and to improper conduct. They were filled with all manner of wickedness"—and Paul proceeds with a list of small *s* "sins": "full of envy, murder, strife, deceit, malignity," and so on (Rom 1:18–32).

In short, sin is not simply wrongdoing that calls for punishment; sin is rooted in an embraced falsehood that cannot be sustained. It is the attempt to live without God, though God is the source and sustainer of all life. It is the attempt to live as though God did not exist—when all our contingent existences are derived from, and dependent on, his necessary existence: "All that borrows life from Thee is ever in Thy care" (Isaac Watts). If God in his mercy sustains life-denying life for a time, it remains the case that life-denying life cannot go on forever. The day will come when the God by whom we live will no longer be denied, when "the earth will be filled with the knowledge of the glory of the LORD as the waters cover the sea" (Hab 2:14).

---

1. Biblical quotations are taken from the Revised Standard Version, except where otherwise indicated.

> By myself I have sworn,
> from my mouth has gone forth in righteousness
> a word that shall not return:
> "To me every knee shall bow,
> every tongue shall swear."
> Only in the LORD, it shall be said of me,
> are righteousness and strength;
> to him shall come and be ashamed,
> all who were incensed against him. (Isa 45:23–24)

Put differently: If God is all-good, all-knowing, and all-powerful, we can explain the temporary existence of evil by saying that God saw fit to make creatures with minds and wills of their own, creatures who then misused the gifts they were given. What remains inconceivable, in a universe created by an all-good, all-knowing, and all-powerful God, is that God's purposes should finally be frustrated, that evil should have the last word: rather, at some point, God in his goodness, wisdom, and power will see to it that goodness, beauty, and truth prevail, and that all that is evil, deforming, and false is done away. However we understand Scripture's various depictions of how that transformation will take place, the transformation itself is inevitable.

So far, then, the general framework for Scripture's summons to repentance.

Implications of the Framework

Four implications critical to our subject may be drawn from the general framework I have just outlined. First, repentance has its place, its necessary place, throughout the whole period from the sin of Adam and Eve until the day when God's name is universally hallowed, his kingdom come, and his will done on earth as it is in heaven. It is true that BC, in the period before the coming of Christ, the summons to repentance was generally directed to the people of Israel, the people God had chosen for himself and for his redemptive purposes. Paul in Athens, in Acts 17, can speak of God overlooking "the times of [pagan] ignorance," though he now commands all people everywhere to repent (Acts 17:30). In Lystra, in Acts 14, Paul speaks of how God "in past generations . . . allowed all the nations to walk in their own ways," though "he did not leave himself without witness, for he did good and gave [them] from heaven rains and fruitful seasons, satisfying [their] hearts with food and gladness" (Acts 14:16–17). Yet even BC, even before Christ, the heathen people of Nineveh were delivered from prophesied doom when, at the preaching of Jonah, they repented of their evil (John 3:1–10; Matt 12:41). To Israel before Christ, God sent "all [his] servants the prophets, sending them persistently, saying, 'Turn now every one of you from his evil way, and amend your doings, and do not go after other gods to serve them, and then you shall dwell in the land which I gave to you and your fathers'" (Jer 35:15). That was BC, before Christ. In the present age, as we have seen, God commands everyone everywhere to repent (Acts 17:30). God has exalted Christ to his own right hand "to give repentance to Israel and forgiveness of sins": so Acts 5:31. A few chapters later on, the Jerusalem saints, to their surprise, come to recognize that "to the Gentiles also God has granted repentance unto life" (Acts 11:18). That God has "granted repentance" suggests to some that repentance, like faith, is a gift given the elect by irresistible divine grace; but since, according to the narrative of Acts, Israel largely proved resistant, the divine gift must be that of the possibility, the invitation, the opportunity to repent. That possibility, that invitation, that opportunity is now extended to all, Israel and the gentiles alike—for the time being. The heavens must "receive" Christ "until the time for establishing all that God spoke by the mouth of his holy prophets from of old"; in the meantime, summons is given to "repent" and "turn again, that your sins may be blotted out" (Acts 3:19–21).

Many have labeled the present age the "age of grace." It is that, to be sure: "Behold, now is the acceptable time; behold, now is the day of salvation" (2 Cor 6:2). But we could designate it equally well the "age of repentance." Scripture makes it clear that God allows the anomaly of a world rebelling against its Maker precisely in order to give opportunity to repent. Jesus speaks in a parable of a barren fig tree spared for yet another year in the hope that it may yet bear fruit (Luke 13:6–9); Israel's repentance is in view. Paul writes that God's "kindness and forbearance and patience" are meant to "lead [sinners] to repentance" (Rom 2:4). Second Peter explains the apparent delay of the day of the Lord in similar terms: "The Lord is not slow about his promise as some count slowness, but is forbearing toward you, not wishing that any should perish, but that all should reach repentance" (2 Pet 3:9).

This first, then: the present age—and, indeed, the whole period from Adam until the eschaton—is the age of repentance: the age where repentance is needed, called for, and still a possibility.

A second implication that follows from the general framework I described above is that true repentance necessarily involves a return to, and acknowledgment of, the God against whom all small *s* "sins" are ultimately committed, and against whom capital *S* "Sin," the refusal to acknowledge God, is essentially directed. Individuals, groups, institutions, corporations, and societies all have cause for repentance. They may find it self-servingly prudent or even a matter of conscience to confess wrongs done to others and to speak the language of repentance. But unless God is acknowledged as offended by our sins, and unless repentance includes a turning from sin *to God* in prayers for mercy and a commitment to obey and trust God, then repentance, as Scripture speaks of repentance, has not taken place. The fundamental Sin has not been addressed. The message Paul brought to Jews and Gentiles alike was one of "repentance *to God* and of faith in our Lord Jesus Christ" (Acts 20:21). He "declared first to those at Damascus, then at Jerusalem and throughout all the country of Judea, and also to the Gentiles, that they should *repent and turn to God* and perform deeds worthy of their repentance" (Acts 26:20). One of the two Hebrew verbs for repentance in the Old Testament means literally "to turn" or "return," and in the vast majority of its Old Testament usages, it has no religious significance: we "turn," or "return," many times every day to all manner of activities or places. But when the verb means "repent," the point is that sin must be turned *from*, and God turned *to*, if disaster is to be averted or, disaster having taken place, restoration is to occur.

> When you are in tribulation, ... you will *return to the LORD* your God and obey his voice, for the LORD your God is a merciful God. (Deut 4:30–31)
>
> *Turn to me* and be saved, all the ends of the earth! For I am God and there is no other. (Isa 45:22)
>
> Seek the LORD while he may be found,
> call upon him while he is near;
> let the wicked forsake his way,
> and the unrighteous man his thoughts;
> let him *return to the LORD*, that he may have mercy upon him,
> and to our God, for he will abundantly pardon. (Isa 55:6–7)

Repentance and Forgiveness

Paul distinguishes worldly grief, which leads only to death, from godly grief, which leads to repentance and salvation. Many of us know the experience that elicited from Paul his discussion of the two kinds of grief. He had written a letter to the Corinthians, put it in the mailbox (so to speak), then wished he could get it back again. He regretted, for a time, that he had sent the letter, fearing it would hurt the Corinthians and wondering what might follow. But when he learned that the letter had resulted in a *godly* grief, he could rejoice, because *godly* grief leads to repentance that in turn leads to salvation; playing on words, Paul notes that such repentance leaves no cause for regret (2 Cor 7:8–10); no need to repent of repentance. The point is this. All human beings experience regret. But regret in itself leads nowhere. Repentance goes beyond regret in acknowledging that God has been offended, in confessing one's sin in the first place to God, and in being accompanied by a commitment henceforth to walk in God's ways. Such is repentance as Scripture envisages it: repentance that leads to life.

Third implication: I mentioned above texts in Acts that speak of God *granting* repentance; they appear to mean that God gave the opportunity to repent. The point to be underlined here is that this in itself is no mean gift, nor one to be presumed upon. "It is of the LORD's mercies that we are not consumed" (Lam 3:22, KJV). "He does not deal with us according to our sins, nor requite us according to our iniquities" (Ps 103:10). He is "a God merciful and gracious, slow to anger and abounding in steadfast love and faithfulness" (Exod 34:6). The possibility, the invitation, the opportunity to repent are themselves gifts of God's grace, his unmerited favor. And they are not to be taken for granted. Indeed, they are what we call "limited time offers." "Seek the LORD *while he may be found*" (Isa 55:6). Not only are the days of our years threescore years and ten, or perhaps fourscore years; not only does the age of repentance itself have its boundaries and point of termination; Scripture also tells of hardened souls for whom the possibility of repentance is no longer held open even though, physically speaking, they are still alive. Isaiah's message was to

> make the heart of this people fat,
> and their ears heavy,
> and shut their eyes;
> lest they see with their eyes,
> and hear with their ears,
> and understand with their hearts,
> and turn and be healed. (Isa 6:10)

Jeremiah was told not to pray for the welfare of his people, since God had determined to consume them (Jer 14:11–12; cf. Ezek 24:14). Hebrews strikingly finds no possibility of repentance for those once enlightened who have "spurned the Son of God" and crucified him "on their own account" (Heb 6:4–8; 10:26–31), citing the example of Esau, who "found no chance to repent, though he sought it with tears" (12:17). God's "mercies never come to an end" (Lam 3:22), but death brings an end to the possibility of availing ourselves of those mercies. And hardened sinners may reach *that* end even before the end of their days. The very goodness of God that gives sinners the opportunity to repent cannot, in the end, allow the determined *un*repentant to continue perverting God's creation.

Fourth implication, self-evident by this point but worth underlining nonetheless. The grace God offers to sinners who repent must not be confused with mere acceptance of sinners or a benign divine indifference to sin. God commands everyone everywhere to repent because he is *good*, and in his *goodness* is determined to root out all that is *evil* from his creation. The God who is merely *nice*, who is all about acceptance, who accepts everyone just as they are, is not the God of the Bible.[2] God is in the business of making all things good, an undertaking that cannot allow sinners to go on forever in their sin. He is in the business of transforming sinners, not patting them on the back. "Be sure of this, that no fornicator or impure person, or one who is greedy (that is, an idolater), has any inheritance in the kingdom of Christ and of God. Let no one deceive you with empty words, for because of these things the wrath of God comes on those who are disobedient" (Eph 5:5–6, NRSV). For our purposes, that single text will serve to represent a thousand others that could be cited.

So let me sum up the implications that, I suggest, follow from Scripture's framework of creation, sin, redemption, and restoration.

1. We live in an age in which repentance is both necessary and possible, an age that began with the sin of Adam and Eve and that will reach its end at the eschaton, when God puts all things right.
2. True repentance necessarily involves a turning from sin *to God* in confession, trust, and obedience.

---

2. See chapter 3 ("Divine Goodness") in C. S. Lewis's *The Problem of Pain* (London: Geoffrey Bles, 1940).

3. The possibility of repentance, the invitation to repent together with the assurance of forgiveness for those who truly do so, are gifts of God's grace not to be presumed upon.

4. The grace of God is offered the vilest offenders, but to the end that they may be made good. Scripture's message of repentance and forgiveness, and of the grace of God that makes repentance and forgiveness possible for sinners, presupposes the reality of human sin and God's necessary opposition to it.

A Curious Question

Before we turn from these general considerations to what Scripture says about repentance in a few specific contexts, I want to raise a question that is only indirectly, but still importantly, related to our topic: Does God himself repent? The immediate and obvious answer is no, if by repentance we mean turning from sin to God: God has no sin to turn from, and he can hardly turn to himself. But in addition to the verb whose basic meaning is "to turn" or "return," the Hebrew Old Testament often uses a second verb for repentance, a verb whose basic meaning is "to be sorry," "to regret," "to rue." And such regret, "repentance" in this sense, is both said categorically to be something incompatible with the divine nature *and* to be something that human behavior brings God to experience.

I leave it to you how agitated you choose to be over the anthropomorphisms contained in such language. Origen linked the whole process of maturing in faith to an increased understanding of God's spiritual nature: one starts by reading Scripture literally, including its anthropomorphic ways of speaking of God, then gradually rises to a better understanding of the God who is Spirit. Luther, on the other hand, chose to delight in Scripture's anthropomorphisms.

> Most delightful are the descriptions of this sort, when Scripture speaks about God as if He were a human being and attributes to Him all human qualities, namely, that He converses with us in a friendly manner and about matters similar to those which human beings discuss; that He is glad, is sad, and suffers like a human being.[3]

---

3. Martin Luther, *Luther's Works*, edited by Jaroslav Pelikan and Helmut T. Lehmann (St. Louis: Concordia, 1955–86) 4.133.

Not even the language of God repenting troubled him.

> It is superfluous to enter on the subtle question here how God can repent, turn from and regret His anger, since He is unchangeable. Some people are deeply concerned about this: they complicate the matter for themselves unnecessarily.[4]

No one, Luther thought, is really deceived by such language. And in any case, what other way do we have to speak about God? God can only reveal himself "in some such veil or wrapper": therefore, when we embrace the "wrapper" (i.e., Scripture's anthropomorphic language of God), we are embracing God as God has chosen to reveal himself.[5] We cannot look on God in his "naked majesty."[6] No one is more insistent than Luther on the necessity of clinging to God as God has revealed himself: "You cannot grasp God in Himself, unless perchance you want a consuming fire."[7]

Leaving Origen and Luther behind us, and assuming that we may discern something of the divine intent from the nature of Scripture, it is worth pondering that God deems it better for us to understand his profound engagement with his creatures in anthropomorphic ways than to risk our mistaking divine transcendence for divine indifference. Bearing that in mind, and perhaps expressing my preference in this case for Luther's counsel over that of Origen, I will speak in what follows, with Scripture, of God's grief, his regret, his repenting.

We turn first, however, to the categorical denials that God "repents."

> God is not man, that he should lie,
> or the son of a man, that he should repent.
> Has he said, and will he not do it?
> Or has he spoken, and will he not fulfil it? (Num 23:19, RSV)

> The Glory of Israel will not lie or repent; for he is not a man, that he should repent. (1 Sam 15:28–29, RSV)

In the context of the first quotation, Balak has attempted to persuade Balaam to curse Israel. Balaam replies that God's determination to bless Israel cannot be altered: God cannot be induced to change what he has

---

4. *Luther's Works* 19.88; cf. 33.71.
5. *Luther's Works* 1.14–15.
6. *Luther's Works* 16.54.
7. *Luther's Works* 16.55. See the discussion of Origen and Luther on Scripture in Stephen Westerholm and Martin Westerholm, *Reading Sacred Scripture: Voices from the History of Biblical Interpretation* (Grand Rapids: Eerdmans, 2016), 67–100, 198–239.

resolved upon doing. The point in the second text is the same: the Lord's decision to replace Saul as king with his better is not one God can be induced to revoke. In both texts, the prerogative proverbially allowed the female sex of changing one's mind is portrayed as a universal *human* weakness, but not one to which God is subject.

Fair enough, and straightforward enough, one would have thought. "The LORD hath sworn, and will not repent" (Ps 110:4, KJV). "The gifts and the call of God are irrevocable" (Rom 11:29). With "the Father of lights," James tells us, "there is no variation or shadow due to change" (Jas 1:17). God is God. He does not change his mind. God does not repent.

Except, of course, for when he does, and there is no shortage of texts that affirm the latter, using the same verb as that found in the categorical denials just cited. God sees the great wickedness by which human beings pollute the earth, and he "regrets," he "rues the fact," he "*repents*" that he made them (Gen 6:5–7). Most strikingly, both immediately before and immediately after the categorical *denial* of 1 Samuel 15:29 that the Lord repents, we are told in verses 11 and 35 of the same chapter that the Lord "repented" that he had made Saul king over Israel. More frequently, we are told that the Lord "repented" in the sense that he decided, after all, *not* to proceed with judgment that he had pronounced or even begun. After the sin of the golden calf, Moses prayed that God would "repent" of the destruction he had announced against his people; as a result, we are told, "The LORD repented of the evil which he thought to do to his people" (Exod 32:12, 14). God "repents" and prevents his angel from continuing the destruction of Jerusalem after David's sin in numbering his subjects (2 Sam 24:16; 1 Chron 21:15; cf. Jer 26:19). In Amos 7, after seeing visions of divine judgment, the prophet Amos twice prayed, "O Lord GOD, forgive, I beseech thee! How can Jacob stand? He is so small!" And twice we are told, "The LORD repented concerning this; 'It shall not be,'" he said (Amos 7:1–6). The people of Nineveh, though given no hope that God would do anything other than destroy their city within forty days, turned from their evil ways with the words, "Who knows, God may yet repent and turn from his fierce anger, so that we perish not?" And we read, "When God saw what they did, how they turned from their evil way, God repented of the evil which he had said he would do to them; and he did it not" (Jonah 3:9–10; cf. Joel 2:12–14). Jeremiah articulates the principle behind all these texts: God is ever ready to repent both of prophesied judgment, if those appointed for destruction turn from their evil, and of prophesied good, if those appointed for blessing turn to evil (Jer 18:5–10; cf. 26:3, 13).

Of the texts that speak of God "repenting," it would be fair to say that this anthropomorphic way of speaking serves to underline God's unchanging commitment to show mercy to sinners who repent, and his willingness to allow his servants, through their prayers, to stand in the gap and to divert, for a time, his wrath from sinners (cf. Ps 106:23; Ezek 22:30). God's announced plans, but not his character, may be altered in the light of alterations in human behavior; still, his compassion and goodness remain constant, expressed in a willingness to forgive the repentant and a determination to oppose what is evil. To repeat the point made earlier: better to grasp in anthropomorphic ways something of God's profound engagement with his creatures than to mistake his transcendence and immutability for indifference.

Old Testament Texts

In what remains, I want us to look at a few texts and contexts in Scripture in which repentance appears prominently. First, from the Old Testament, and I begin with the story and times of Josiah, king of Judah in Jerusalem from 640–609 BC, following the two-year reign of his father Amon and the fifty-five year reign of his grandfather Manasseh. Of Manasseh, the account in 2 Kings has nothing good to say: he "seduced" his people "to do more evil than the nations had done whom the LORD destroyed before the people of Israel." He himself did "things more wicked than all that the Amorites did, who were before him." He "filled Jerusalem from one end to another" with "innocent blood"—including, as tradition would have it, that of the prophet Isaiah (2 Kgs 21:9, 11, 16; Mart. Isa.). Second Chronicles 33 begins its account of Manasseh in exactly the same terms as 2 Kings, but indicates that, when God brought him into distress, "he entreated the favor of the LORD his God and humbled himself greatly before the God of his fathers. He prayed to him, and God received his entreaty" (2 Chron 33:12–13; cf. Pr. Man.). The story of Manasseh thus became, in Judaism, the ultimate proof that God is willing to forgive even the greatest of sinners who repent.

Josiah, on the other hand, is said to have done "what was right in the eyes of the LORD" from the outset of his reign (2 Kgs 22:2). As the temple was being repaired, the "book of the law" was discovered, the content of which must have corresponded to the substance of our book of

Repentance and Forgiveness

Deuteronomy. The book is read to the king. He tears his clothes and sends messengers to Huldah the prophetess to find out if anything can be done to avert divine judgment. Huldah says that judgment is indeed coming, but not until after Josiah's days, since he has humbled himself before the Lord. Josiah proceeds to summon his subjects to Jerusalem, read them the book of the law, and enter, with them, into a covenant to keep God's commandments. He then does everything in his power to banish idolatrous worship from his realm. The narrative in 2 Kings assures us that, Josiah's piety notwithstanding, the anger of the Lord continued to burn against Judah (2 Kgs 22–23).

Several points are worth noting. As normally in Scripture, repentance was evoked by the hearing of God's word. More specifically, repentance was evoked by an awareness, brought by the word of God, of pending judgment. That pronouncements of pending judgment brought repentance was *not* the experience of most prophets, major and minor alike; but it happened here, and in the case of the heathen city of Nineveh. Furthermore, repentance in the case of Israel (or Judah) involved a return to the commandments of God with which they had been entrusted and to faithfulness to the covenant God had entered with their forebears at Mount Sinai. Finally, we note, though 2 Kings does not, that the national reformation that Josiah attempted to bring about occurred during the activity of the prophet Jeremiah; and though Jeremiah had high praise for Josiah himself (Jer 22:15–16), he appears to have regarded the national reformation as superficial. In words explicitly dated to the time of Josiah, Jeremiah noted that, even though the southern kingdom of Judah was aware that the idolatry of her sister to the north had led to its banishment, she herself "did not return to [God] with her whole heart, but in pretense" (Jer 3:10). Not all who lament, repent.

Jeremiah 34 tells of another incident of sham repentance. At a time when the city was under siege, King Zedekiah entered a covenant with the people of Jerusalem to free their Hebrew slaves, as required by a long disregarded provision of Mosaic law. They "repented and did what was right in [God's] eyes by proclaiming liberty, each to his neighbor" (Jer 34:15). But as soon as the siege was lifted and the immediate crisis had passed, they reverted to form and took back the very slaves they had released.

Normally, it is the word of God that evokes repentance; but Scripture also indicates that disasters themselves, interpreted as divine judgment, at least *ought* to lead to repentance. Generally, however, the story of the Old Testament is that even the experience of divine judgment fails to move hardhearted sinners to repentance. As we have just seen, Judah showed no true repentance even after her sister was sent into exile. Hardness of heart kept Pharaoh from heeding God's word as plague after plague devastated his land. And in one of the most powerful passages in all of Scripture, the God of Amos lists a series of increasingly destructive judgments he had sent upon the people of Israel, adding after each description, "yet you did not return to me. . . . Therefore, . . . prepare to meet your God, O Israel!" (Amos 4:6–12).

Joel finds in a devastating plague of locusts occasion to summon his people to repentance (Joel 1:1—2:17). At the same time, he is aware that rituals of repentance can be enacted without the heart's engagement, and hence to no purpose: "'Yet even now,' says the LORD, 'return to me with all your heart, . . . and rend your hearts and not your garments'" (Joel 2:12—13). Similarly, Isaiah 58 denounces rituals of repentance conducted by those who continue to oppress their workers. Words themselves are not enough; neither are external rites of penitence. The whole chapter merits quotation, though the following verses convey the essence of the prophet's message.

> Is not this the fast that I choose:
> to loose the bonds of injustice,
> to undo the thongs of the yoke,
> to let the oppressed go free,
> and to break every yoke?
> Is it not to share your bread with the hungry,
> and bring the homeless poor into your house;
> when you see the naked, to cover them,
> and not to hide yourself from your own kin?
> Then your light shall break forth like the dawn,
> and your healing shall spring up quickly;
> your righteousness shall go before you,
> the glory of the LORD shall be your rear guard.
> Then you shall call, and the LORD will answer;
> you shall cry for help, and he will say, Here I am. (Isa 58:6-9)

I debated whether we should look at Old Testament texts in which a servant of God confesses the sins of his people and pleads for God's mercy. Daniel 9 contains such a prayer, as does Nehemiah 9, the end of Isaiah 63, and all of 64. These (and others like them) are wonderful and moving

Repentance and Forgiveness

passages of Scripture, but in this context it must be noted that they do not really signal repentance, a turning to God from sin, on the part of the faithful petitioner, or of those on whose behalf confession is made and for whom God's mercy is implored. I spoke earlier of righteous servants of God who stood in the gap and diverted, through their prayers, God's judgment for a time from sinners. This is clearly a good thing—but it cannot, I think, be called repentance.

Before we turn to New Testament texts, let me remind you of aspects of Old Testament repentance that will contrast with what we find in the New. I have already noted that, BC, the summons to repentance was largely directed to Israel, whereas, AD, it is issued to Israel and the gentiles alike, though starting with the former. I have also noted how repentance is often urged in the light of pending judgment. That is true in Old Testament and New Testament alike, though in the Old Testament, the judgment is typically envisaged as taking place within history—for example, conquest by the Assyrians or Babylonians—whereas in the New Testament, the judgment before which repentance is urged is the last judgment marking the end of the age and of history as we know it. Repentance for Israel in the Old Testament meant a looking back, a returning to faithfulness to the commandments given their forebears at Mount Sinai and to the covenant with God that they entered there. In the New Testament, repentance means looking ahead not only to deliverance from the last judgment but also to entrance into God's kingdom.

New Testament Texts

We begin with John the Baptist, forerunner of the Messiah. The Synoptic Baptist looks forward to a Messiah whose "winnowing fork is in his hand, and he will clear his threshing floor and gather his wheat into the granary, but the chaff he will burn with unquenchable fire" (Matt 3:12). He will baptize "with the Holy Spirit and with fire"—presumably, the fire of divine judgment (3:11). The focus, for John, is not backwards; after all, God can raise up children for Abraham from stones. John's attention is forward, looking ahead to the "wrath to come"; indeed, "even now the axe is laid to the root of the trees; every tree therefore that does not bear good fruit is cut down and thrown into the fire" (3:7, 10). With this in view, the first word that the evangelist puts on the mouth of John the Baptist is "Repent!" (3:2).

And John baptized. Those who came out to him in the wilderness "were baptized by him in the river Jordan, confessing their sins" (3:6). He himself spoke of his baptism as a baptism with water "for repentance" (3:11). Mark and Luke indicate that John preached "a baptism of repentance *for the forgiveness of sins*" (Mark 1:4; Luke 3:3). Matthew associates *confession* of sins with John's baptism, but says nothing in this context of sins' forgiveness, perhaps because he believes forgiveness belongs more properly to the activity of Jesus. It is in any case clear that John's baptism was not still another repeatable cleansing from quotidian defilement, but a one-time expression of a resolute act of repentance, preparing for the decisive divine intervention in a sin-defiled world, a judgment by which evil would be banished and righteousness established. Baptism signaled a moral reformation without which the ritual itself was meaningless: "Bear fruit that befits repentance," John declared (Matt 3:8); and in Luke's account, specific examples of such fruit are given: sharing goods with the needy, and acting with integrity in one's daily work (Luke 3:10–14).

To quote John's initial words in the Gospel of Matthew more fully, he came preaching "Repent, for the kingdom of heaven is at hand" (Matt 3:2). The words are the same as the summary of Jesus's proclamation in Matthew 4:17, adapted from Mark's summary in Mark 1:15: "The time is fulfilled, and the kingdom of God is at hand; repent, and believe in the gospel." The coming of God's kingdom, and the conditions for entering it, are the main themes of the message of the Synoptic Jesus. I noted earlier that though the temporary presence of evil in a world created by a God who is good, all-wise, and all-powerful is explicable, in the end God's goodness must prevail, evil must be banished, and righteousness established. Jesus proclaims that God has begun to do precisely that. The process, to be sure, has only begun: the kingdom of God now appears in the (easily overlooked) form of a grain of mustard seed; but from the tiniest of seeds will come a growth so great that birds can nest in its shade (Mark 4:30–32). "If it is by the Spirit of God that I cast out demons, then the kingdom of God has come upon you" (Matt 12:28)—even if its full realization lies in a future for which Jesus's disciples are to pray, "Thy kingdom come" (Matt 6:10). The point for our purposes is that the period between the dawning and the full realization of God's kingdom again constitutes a period in which repentance is both possible and essential if judgment is to be avoided and God's favor is to be enjoyed, here through a share in the blessings of his kingdom. "The kingdom of God is at hand; repent, and believe in the gospel."

Repentance and Forgiveness

The summons to repentance is universal. Jesus dismisses any suggestion that victims of recent disasters were worse sinners than others: "Unless you repent you will all likewise perish" (Luke 13:1–5). John the Baptist spoke metaphorically of the axe already at the root of trees, ready to cut down whatever does not bear fruit; Jesus picks up the metaphor and reaffirms it, though allowing for a delay in its immediate application: "Let [the tree] alone, sir, this year also, till I dig about it and put on manure. And if it bears fruit next year, well and good; but if not, you can cut it down" (Luke 13:8–9). He laments that his contemporaries have failed to take to heart both the message of the ascetic John the Baptist and that of "the friend of tax collectors and sinners" (Matt 11:16–19). Not even his mighty works have led to the repentance needed for deliverance on the day of judgment: "Woe to you, Chorazin! woe to you, Bethsaida! for if the mighty works done in you had been done in Tyre and Sidon, they would have repented long ago in sackcloth and ashes. But I tell you, it shall be more tolerable on the day of judgment for Tyre and Sidon than for you" (Matt 11:21–22). Or again: "The people of Nineveh will rise up at the judgment with this generation and condemn it, because they repented at the proclamation of Jonah, and see, something greater than Jonah is here!" (Matt 12:41, NRSV).

Some of Jesus's contemporaries were offended by Jesus's association with notoriously sinful people: tax collectors, prostitutes, and the like. Not even the most notoriously sinful were excluded from Jesus's summons to repentance, faith, and God's kingdom. The sick are those in obvious need of the physician (Mark 2:17). The prodigal son retains a place in the Father's love and is welcomed home (Luke 15:11–32). But to repeat a point made earlier: the welcome Jesus offered to the most despised of sinners should not be confused with tolerating, even accepting, a sinful lifestyle. Matthew, though a tax collector, was invited to be Jesus's disciple; but he left all to follow Jesus, and was soon to learn, if he did not know already, the rigorous demands of discipleship (Matt 9:9). The prodigal son was welcomed back to the Father's home, but he first had to leave the far country. Jesus speaks of the great joy in heaven over a single sinner who repents (Luke 15:7, 10); the joy—note well—is occasioned by the sinner's *repentance*.

I want to look in a little more detail at a narrative sequence in Matthew 21. The first part of the sequence, Matthew 21:23–27, is found in Mark and Luke as well. After cleansing the temple, Jesus is approached by "the chief priests and the elders of the people" with a question: "By what authority are you doing these things, and who gave you this authority?" Jesus, choosing to answer the question indirectly rather than directly, responds with a counter-question: Was the baptism of John a divine or merely human initiative? Jesus's interlocutors find themselves in a dilemma: they cannot allow that John was divinely commissioned without showing themselves to be guilty of indifference or even resistance to God's messenger; they also cannot dismiss John's claims to be God's messenger without risking popular disfavor. They lamely reply, "We don't know." Given that response to his question, Jesus refuses to directly answer theirs.

In effect, his answer has already been given, though indirectly. His counter-question is not a clever tactical device to avoid answering. His indirect answer is, "If you are prepared to respond to John the Baptist's divine message, then you will recognize and respond to mine as well. But with those not prepared to acknowledge John's divine authority, there is no point in discussing mine." Note that, when Jesus's interlocutors deliberate among themselves, the question of whether John's inspiration was divine or human is not even raised; the *truth* about John is of no interest to them. Their only concern is how they will *appear* before others if they give *this* answer or *that*. Again, there is no point in discussing the authority of God's spokespeople with those unprepared to submit to God's will, those whose only concern is their reputation on earth: "How *can* you believe, who receive glory from one another and do not seek the glory that comes from the only God?" (John 5:44).

In Matthew's Gospel, Jesus then continues with the parable of two sons, both asked to go and work in their father's vineyard. One barefacedly refused, but then "repented" and went. The other respectfully agreed, but did not go. The former did the father's will. So the tax collectors and prostitutes, whose initial way of life represented a refusal of God's will, *repented and believed* John the Baptist; religious leaders, whose way of life suggested a readiness to submit to God's will, turned, at the crucial moment, a deaf ear to his messenger. Jesus thereby answers his own question about the authority of John, and, implicitly, the question about his own.

The link in this passage between repentance and faith (Matt 21:32) is an important one, and found elsewhere as well. I have already cited Mark 1:15: "The kingdom of God is at hand; repent, and believe the gospel." *Repent and believe.* Paul, in Acts, speaks of "repentance to God *and* of faith in our Lord Jesus Christ" (Acts 20:21); Hebrews, "of repentance from dead works and of faith toward God" (Heb 6:1). Repentance by sinners is always in order, and a guilty conscience is in itself sufficient grounds for repentance;

Repentance and Forgiveness

but in Scripture a motive for repentance may be found in displays of divine power, in fear of coming judgment, or in the hope of enjoying divine favor. The repentance to which Jesus summons is accompanied by all three forms of motivation, though each requires a response of faith. It is *faith* that sees in the mighty works of Jesus the power of God's kingdom; *faith* repentantly accepts the grace and forgiveness Jesus offers, in the hope of eternal life. As Matthew Henry (on Mark 1:15) puts it: "We must not think either that reforming our lives will save us without trusting in the righteousness and grace of Christ, or that trusting in Christ will save us without the reformation of our hearts and lives. Repentance will quicken faith, and faith will make repentance evangelical."[8]

Before we leave the Synoptic Gospels, one more passage, this time in Luke, requires attention. According to Luke 17:3–4, Jesus said to his disciples: "Take heed to yourselves: if your brother or sister sins, rebuke them, and if they repent, forgive them; and if they sin against you seven times in the day, and turn to you seven times, and say, 'I repent,' you must forgive them" (RSV, modified). The point is an essential part of Jesus's message—so essential that it is included even in the Lord's prayer: "Forgive us our debts, as we also have forgiven our debtors" (Matt 6:12). Those forgiven by the God against whom they have sinned must extend forgiveness to all who sin against them (cf. Eph. 4:32).

Outside the Synoptic Gospels, repentance is a significant theme in the Acts of the Apostles and the book of Revelation. Before we look at these texts, however, it is worth thinking for a moment about the complete absence of any reference to repentance in the Gospel or Epistles of John, and the almost complete absence in the Paulines.[9] Of course, the epistles of both Paul and John were directed to those who had already been baptized into Christ Jesus, so there was no place in these texts for a summons to the repentance that marks conversion. And Paul does, on two occasions, speak of the need for the Corinthian believers to repent of particular sins (2 Cor 7:9, 10; 12:21). Most importantly, we should note that repentance signals a break with one's sinful past, and that in the writings of neither Paul nor John is that need overlooked or minimized; if anything, it is spoken of in terms more categorical than repentance itself. In John's Gospel, all that is born of the flesh is flesh. Entrance into God's kingdom requires a new

---

8. Matthew Henry, *Matthew Henry's Commentary on the Whole Bible*, 6 vols (Peabody: Hendrickson, 1991), 5:367.

9. But cf. the discussion of Rom 2:4; 2 Cor 7:8–10 above. Note also 2 Tim 2:25.

birth in the Spirit of those born of the flesh—that is, of all human beings (John 3:1–7). For Paul, all human beings are born in Adam—born, that is, in sin—and subject to condemnation; what is required for justification and life is a death, with Christ, to the old way of life and a rising, with Christ, to a new life lived for God (Romans 5–6). A second birth, on the one hand; death and resurrection, on the other; even more than the language of repentance, the language adopted by John and Paul calls for a radical break with the past and the beginnings of a new life. Flesh itself can effect neither the break nor the beginning; both are possible only through the work of God's Spirit.

But to return to Acts and Revelation. The Gospel of Luke ends with the resurrected Jesus opening the minds of his disciples so that they could "understand the scriptures": "Thus it is written, that the Christ should suffer and on the third day rise from the dead, and that repentance and forgiveness of sins should be preached in his name to all nations, beginning from Jerusalem" (Luke 24:45–47). The verses clearly set forth the agenda for "Luke's Story of Jesus: the Sequel," and in Acts, we see the carrying out of the agenda. In the early chapters, "repentance [is given] to Israel and forgiveness of sins" (Acts 5:31)—meaning, as we have seen, that Israel is given opportunity to repent and know the forgiveness of its sins. The latter are hardly confined to the rejection of their Messiah, though that seems the primary focus both in Peter's address on the day of Pentecost in Acts 2, and when he addresses astonished crowds after healing a lame man in Acts 3. In both cases, the call for repentance follows immediately upon reference to God's exaltation of the very Jesus "whom you crucified" (Acts 2:36, 38; 3:14–15, 19). Repentance in these texts is more or less equated with conversion to Christianity, though, to be sure, repentance stresses the turning from sin necessarily involved, together with faith in Christ, in the process. "Repent, and be baptized every one of you in the name of Jesus Christ for the forgiveness of your sins; and you shall receive the gift of the Holy Spirit" (2:38). In later chapters, as we have seen, "repentance unto life" is also given to the Gentiles (11:18), Paul speaks of God's command to all people everywhere to repent (17:30), and summarizes his ministry as "testifying both to Jews and Greeks of repentance to God and of faith in our Lord Jesus Christ" (20:21; cf. 26:20). Gentile idolatry provides the primary, though of course not the exclusive, occasion for their repentance (17:22–31).

Suitably enough, the book of Revelation speaks of repentance in ways that sum up much of what we have seen on the theme in other parts of

Repentance and Forgiveness

Scripture. Wherever there is sin, there is need for repentance. In seven letters sent to seven churches, fault is found with five of the churches, and in each case, repentance is urged (Rev 2:5, 16, 21–22; 3:3, 19). That disasters brought on by divine judgment provide an occasion for repentance, but that human defiance of God typically persists even under these circumstances proves true during the woes plaguing humankind at the end of the age: "The rest of humankind, who were not killed by these plagues, did not repent of the works of their hands or give up worshiping demons and idols . . . and they did not repent of their murders or their sorceries or their fornications or their thefts" (9:20–21, NRSV; cf. 16:9, 11). That there comes a point where repentance is no longer a possibility for hardened sinners is underlined in the Bible's final chapter: "Let the evildoer still do evil, and the filthy still be filthy, and the righteous still do right, and the holy still be holy" (22:11). Above all, of course, we see in Revelation the inevitable end of a world in rebellion against its good, all-wise, and all-powerful Maker. Evil is permitted its day, but that day has an end; so, too, does the age of repentance. In the end, the goodness, wisdom, and power of God combine to make inevitable the banishing of all that is evil, and a world made new in which dwells righteousness.

2

A Psycho-theological Reading of Repentance and Forgiveness in Judaism and Christianity

Ellen T. Charry

IN APPROACHING REPENTANCE AND forgiveness in Judaism and Christianity we necessarily begin by identifying discontinuities and dispelling understandable but imprecise generalizations in order to promote maximal clarity and understanding. So I begin with three caveats:

1. Ancient Israelite religion, as depicted in the Older Testament, is not Judaism.
2. Christianity is not the "daughter" of Judaism. Both developed more or less contemporaneously over a period of centuries. Siblings is a more appropriate metaphor.
3. Christianity offers "salvation" = spiritual well-being; Judaism offers community. Western Christianity ties salvation to repentance and forgiveness while Judaism does not. Therefore, repentance and forgiveness do not function comparably in the two traditions.

To begin this discussion, I will assume that the first two caveats are readily understood and elaborate only the last: second-millennium Western Christianity offers "salvation," or spiritual well-being resulting from

Repentance and Forgiveness

deliverance from sin and its consequences. Judaism offers community; repentance and forgiveness do not function comparably in the two traditions. I begin with the last phrase: "the two traditions." Here, on the Christian side, I have in mind a moderate modern Western Christian mindset with an Anglican bent that I hope is recognizable. On the Jewish side, I will have in mind classical Judaism, that is classical Judaism as it developed after 70 CE that built on the earlier Pharisaic Judaism that we find reflected in the Younger Testament and the Mishnah[1] written and compiled more or less contemporaneously in the first and second Christian centuries so-called and developed by rabbinic Judaism that is roughly contemporaneous with the Patristic Age.

These two works, the Mishnah and the Younger Testament, both claim to be interpreting Scripture (the Torah, and the prophets [and the psalms]), but in that process redefine it in quite different ways with radically different results. Perhaps 40 percent of the Younger Testament is citations from or allusions to Scripture. Indeed, Paul was fashioning Pauline Judaism. The author of Matthew was fashioning Matthean Judaism. The author of John was fashioning Johannine Judaism. The author of Hebrews was fashioning another version of Judaism. The Mishnah was fashioning Mishnaic Judaism. With the exception of Pauline Judaism, these were all after 70 CE. Paul set the terms for Christianity when he transformed the humiliating death of Jesus into a saving, that is, well-being-producing event (1 Cor 1:17–31). Christianity became a religion that offers personal spiritual repair (salvation) to those who he thinks need it: Jews and Greeks. Needing salvation means various things: atonement for or forgiveness of sin, relatedness to God, belonging to God's covenant with Israel, all of which are different, yet may now run together in Christian sensibility. Paul himself may have thought of the word *euangelium* (good news) as an umbrella term, but it took on a specific and somewhat narrow scope in the West by focusing on forgiveness of sins as atonement.

---

1. Mishnah means "study by repetition." First major compilation of the Oral Torah, edited by Rabbi Judah "the Prince" ca. 200 CE, codified during the crisis of the disastrous and final defeat of the Jews at the hands of the Roman army in 135 CE that expelled Jews from Jerusalem. It has six major sections, or "orders," each subdivided into tractates totaling sixty-three in number. It contains Jewish civil law, domestic law, religious law, and liturgical norms. It is the result of oral discussion by legal scholars interpreting precepts from the Pentateuch. It is written in Hebrew. There are allusions to and paraphrasing of Mishnaic texts in the Younger Testament.

Mishnaic Judaism, on the other hand, some of which took shape before and some after 70 CE, sought to preserve the sacred memory of the Jerusalem cult while at the same time transforming that way of constituting obedience to Scripture for an agrarian society seeking to adhere to Mosaic teaching after the disastrous wars with Rome decimated Jewish identity, religion and community. The Mishnah primarily interprets selected passages from the prescriptive material of the Pentateuch from about Exodus 20 through Deuteronomy. The Mishnah became the definitive Jewish interpretation of Scripture, simultaneously elevating this material above other scriptural texts and subordinating it to itself. While atonement is the focus in much of Leviticus and Numbers, the Mishnah did not concentrate on it. It was more interested in the sections pertaining to family law, agricultural practices, civil law, and purity, as these would create harmoniously functioning civil society.

With the Mishnah in place by about 200 CE, classical Judaism further elaborated it through the Palestinian and Babylonian Gemarot[2] (ca. 400 and 500 CE respectively) to create the two Talmudim,[3] two massive compendia of Jewish practice that spell out in minute detail customs governing Jewish civil society in every respect. Rabbinic literature, of course, also interpreted other Scripture texts as well in the Midrashim (written and collated over a millennium), but the legal foundation of the Mishnah and the Gemarot constituted the core, consolidated by 500 CE, at about the same time that orthodox Christianity was determined at the Council of Chalcedon (451 CE).

In the Christian West, baptism became associated with forgiveness of sins as the central accomplishment of the initiatory rite. It was generally assumed that Christians would not sin after baptism and so post-baptismal transgression of moral and practical standards became problematic and had to be dealt with publically in order to promote public welfare. Tertullian (ca. 150–225) set the stage for the meaning of salvation in the Latin

2. Gemarah means "closure." Discussions and development of passages from the Mishnah that specify Jewish practice. Collected over several hundred years both in Babylonia and Palestine. Texts are appended to the Mishnah for study by generations of Talmud scholars. It is written in Aramaic.

3. Talmud means "learning." Extending to many volumes, it is the body of Jewish civil and ceremonial law and legend comprising the Mishnah and the Gemarah. There are two versions of the Talmud: the Babylonian Talmud (which dates from the fifth century AD but includes earlier material) and the earlier Palestinian or Jerusalem Talmud. The Bablyonian Talmud is more authoritative and indicates how Judaism adapted to diaspora conditions.

Repentance and Forgiveness

West with his short prescriptive treatise *On Penance*.[4] The assumption of the treatise is that Christians do not sin. This marks them off from pagans. Baptism is considered the conclusion of a period of repentant self-examination resulting in the forgiveness of sins through the rite. This forgiveness expresses or perhaps even enacts spiritual health or salvation. Baptism, the culmination of a long process of training and self-examination, is a first repentance so that post-baptismal sin constitutes the loss of salvation. Sinning after baptism essentially puts one outside the community of the saved. As Cyprian would hold: there is no salvation outside the church. Therefore, restoration to the holy community and state of personal holiness required a second penance. Tertullian does not know of the modern three-strikes-and-you're-out rule. For him there are but two, baptism and one more. There is only one opportunity for a second chance. The treatise's main contribution to later penitential sacramental practice is the formulation of *exomologesis*, the imposition of penitential practices: sackcloth and ashes, abstention from quality food and drink, fasting, confession of sin to the priests, and self-denunciation before the community for a considerable period of time, at the conclusion of which, he seems to say, the person is restored to community.

Psychologically speaking, the public nature of the practices associated with repentance begins with knowledge of the threat of eternal hell that promotes fear of God, that in turn prompts appropriate guilt, regret, self-incrimination, and an openness to recrimination that is understood to be reparative.

Psychological relief is found in the release from fear of divine punishment that *exomologesis* assumes or perhaps assures. Thus, by the beginning of the third so-called Christian century, the Latin West's use of fear and guilt to assure social and moral conformity for the sake of the common good and the welfare of society is articulated, although not yet universally established. It was subsequently developed with formal patterns but never challenged.

Augustinian Christianity further elaborated Paul's soteriological concern for "salvation" in terms of how to deal with sin in order to gain or regain spiritual well-being identified as remission of sin or atonement. Behind this was not only Paul but also John 1:29 that identified Jesus of Nazareth as the "lamb of God," the atoning instrument that replaced the

---

4. Tertullian, *Treatises on Penance: "On Penitence" and "On Purity"*, trans. William P. Le Saint, Ancient Christian Writers 28 (Westminster: Newman, 1959), 14–37.

Jerusalem priesthood just as synagogal worship replaced the sacrificial cult on the Jewish side. There is not a direct scriptural warrant for John's phrase here, although Exodus 12 and Isaiah 53:7 are in the background, along with various Leviticus texts on atoning sacrifice that structured the Jerusalem cult.

With Christians driven to eradicate the guilt of sin via Christ's atoning sacrifice, later contributors to that development were Augustine of Hippo and Christian monasticism, both of whom heavily influenced later Western Christianity. Classical Judaism had nothing comparable; it never identified the fall, sin, atonement or justification as central to one's relationship with God, one's eternal fate, or one's moral health. Let us consider each Christian influence in turn. Although the problem of sin was essential long before him, Augustine of Hippo gave the West the notion of original sin. At that point, sin shifted from being incidental untoward or destructive behavior to being sinfulness: a condition, a psychological pathology, or a symbolic congenital defect, that in modern parlance we might call a character disorder that affects every human being to greater or lesser extent. Judaism knows that all people sin and it has remedies and practices that address it. But Augustine gave us the idea that we are not just sinners but essentially sinful. That exceeds being unable not to sin, according to Augustine, with which Judaism might agree. The Augustinian understanding of sin as *superbia* is often translated as pride or inordinate self-esteem, sometimes oversimplified to selfishness. But if we were to translate it into modern psychological terms, it suggests that everyone is at least mildly narcissistic. Character disorders are quite difficult to treat.

The Eastern Christian tradition also began its narrative with the Christian insistence on sin located in a mythical fall into mortality. But it did not have Augustine's notion of original sin or his doctrine of election that posits that because of the fall everyone deserves divine punishment, and only few are exempt from the punishment they deserve and are elected by God to heaven, making up for the number of angels who fell with Satan. Both Eastern and Western Christian monasticism envision a universal fall based on Genesis 3, although the theme became far more important in the West than in the East. That is, all Christians understand Christianity to be a solution to the diagnosis of a moral flaw in humanity. According to biblical warrant, although world history begins with creation, the Christian story takes Genesis 3, which it labels as "the fall," as its theological point of departure. Monasticism took the fall narrative quite seriously, and the

Western penitential system elaborated the fallenness of humanity and its consequent helplessness before God alleviated it by the penitential sacramental system developed after Tertullian. In some cases, monasticism took extreme measures to combat this character disorder. The influence of monastic spirituality and piety notwithstanding, medieval Western Christianity emphasized the sacramental system and, with Anselm of Canterbury, atonement for sinfulness and sacramental absolution became the pivotal soteriological achievement. Alleviating the guilt and anguish incurred as a result of a universal fall, and the consequent threat of divine punishment preoccupied Western Christian theology and piety thereafter, with atonement soteriology centered on the cross, pressing other understandings of attaining spiritual well-being (salvation) to the margins. In short, Western Christianity became preoccupied with what it took to be a universal debilitating defect in human beings. Pressing for harmonious civil society, Anselm of Canterbury reinforced the psychological power of this imputed universal character failing with the wrath of God. God is so distraught by human sin that we are all deserving of capital punishment (*Cur Deus Homo*). We apparently escape (even though we remain mortal) only because God's mercy overcame God's righteous indignation in the cross.

None of this is present in Judaism. Its understanding of sin is behavioral, not character-based or psychological. It does not posit a universal human nature or common personality, let alone a troubled one. It assumes that people can choose good over evil. It does, however, recognize inclinations toward both good and evil, but does not know of the aching struggle that Augustine's Manichaean heritage gave us of the divided will, the better self pitted against the weaker self. Judaism's question is not "How do I manage given that God is displeased with me and I deserve punishment?" but "How do we best live together in community before God, given scriptural warrants and guidance?" Classical Judaism cares about repentance and forgiveness but without the guilt and anguish that drove some into the desert, others into monasteries, and Martin Luther to despair in search of a gracious God whom he could not find in the church that he knew.

Rabbinic Judaism's basic answer to its own question of how best to ensure civil society is to encourage people to sanctify time and space by blessing and thanking God for creation's gifts. Liturgical prayer and practice sanctify time and space, molding a community of belonging in solidarity with God's good blessings. Perhaps a way of characterizing this difference between the two communities is to suggest that Judaism begins its narrative with Genesis 1, enshrined in the liturgy, and quickly moves to Genesis 12 (God's election of Israel through Abraham), while Christianity begins its creed with Genesis 1 and quickly moves to Matthew 1, or perhaps even Romans 4–5.

I apologize for the long throat-clearing prelude, but it is to be sure that we grasp that when talking about repentance and forgiveness between Judaism and Christianity we are cognizant that they are not offering different solutions to the same question but different solutions to different questions. To oversimplify somewhat, Judaism asks how do we best live in community, and Christianity asks how do we find relief from the threat of divine wrath. Ultimately, however, both traditions, and I suggest all religious heritages, are pressing a common concern: how to craft healthy, socially productive societies.

This may be harder to appreciate in a society like ours that now takes separation of religion and state for granted. It is easier to appreciate if we compare Calvin's Geneva to classical Judaism. Judaism's way is to order society according to accepted standards of worship and practice based on biblical warrant honed generation after generation. Christianity's way is to cultivate humble people, classically motivated by fear of eternal punishment in the Middle Ages in order to promote good behavior. Both heritages ground their approaches in obedience to God, but Western Christianity, shaped by the first psychologist, Augustine of Hippo, centered obedience in humility whilst Judaism, untouched by Augustinian pessimism about human nature, located the source of obedience in customized practice, communal prayer, and liturgical rites. Paul's notion that no one can meet God's standard of obedience (Rom 3:9–12; 7:7–12) simply never took hold among Pharisaic, Mishnaic, or rabbinic Jews. Why would God command what is undoable for us? That not only would be setting us up for failure; it would mock God's graciousness and wisdom.

The Pauline-Lutheran heritage imbued the Christian West with the fear, even the expectation, that no one can live obediently, and therefore everyone must constantly seek guilt-reducing reassurance through sacramental assignation of divine forgiveness in order to maintain psychological stability through trust in one's salvation. When psychological relief through the assurance of pardon by a priest is achieved, as the medieval sacramental system enabled it individually, now residually practiced in Protestantism as pronounced by an ordained minister during public worship, or by throwing oneself directly on the grace of God in Christ without sacerdotal intervention, as Luther found helpful, one can rest from the struggle of being tossed from consolation to desolation (as Julian of Norwich put it) and back again. Dante and John Bunyan both offer versions of this lifelong struggle to rest in relief from guilt at deserved divine wrath by clinging to God's grace. All knew that anxiety has a way of creeping back up on one despite believing that one is accepted by God.

For its part, Judaism too knows the tension between divine judgment and divine mercy, but aside from Yom Kippur (Lev 16:29–34; 23:26–32) does not dramatize it for daily living as the Western Christian penitential system did, although other fast days and penitential practices throughout the Jewish liturgical year keep the concern alive.

With this considerable preamble that argues that we do not have a symmetrical playing field here, I turn to the body of this examination of repentance and forgiveness in Judaism and Christianity beginning with Scripture. Then I will explore how penitential need was worked out and finally compare and contrast these developments for conversation between Christians and Jews today. The thesis here, if there is one, is that these two great religious heritages offer one another refreshing perspectives on themselves precisely because they address common concerns rather differently.

Scriptural Foundations of Repentance and Forgiveness

Even as we approach this topic, we encounter another significant asymmetry besetting Christian-Jewish conversation. Christianity and Judaism only partly share a common Scripture. The Hebrew Bible is the whole Bible for Judaism, but only part of and for many only a preface to the Christian Bible, whose primary interest lies elsewhere, as Christian scriptural interpretation of the Older Testament has amply demonstrated.

Here we must again proceed cautiously, recognizing that "the Bible" not only is a different entity for Christianity and for Judaism, but functions differently for them as well. The Christian Bible is central for the former, especially for Protestantism and subsequent interpreters of the tradition who seek its guidance and inspiration. For the latter, however, the Jewish Bible may be the building block of the later tradition, but historically speaking, access to it has been through rabbinic interpretation, much as the Roman Church accessed Scripture through theological interpretation and canon law for centuries. While ancient Jewish hermeneutics sought divine guidance in every word, Christians often interpreted Scripture christologically, beginning with Paul. Indeed, while the Christian Bible is Scripture for Christianity, the Jewish Bible plus the Mishnah and the Gemarah/Talmud together function authoritatively for Judaism. Customary terms for this pairing are the Written Torah (which means "teaching," not "law") and the Oral Torah respectively. While Protestant Christianity put Scripture into the hands of the laity once printing made books widely available, classical Judaism delegated interpretation to authorized leaders for the welfare of the community. The Jewish Bible is the national literature of the Jewish people as much as it is divine revelation. It is to serve the community's needs wherever it may find itself. The Mishnah represents the emergence of Pharisaic Judaism focused on an agrarian life, while the Jewish Bible articulates a semi-nomadic life and the history that focuses it. The Jewish people's transformation into an urban way of life warranted yet another transformation of its sacred writ. With this further caveat in mind, let us proceed to the biblical foundations of repentance and forgiveness that the traditions share.

Vicarious atonement as the means of remediation of sin comes to Judaism and Christianity primarily through the sacerdotal ministrations depicted throughout Leviticus and, to a lesser extent, Numbers. Jews accepted the destruction of the temple by Rome in 70 CE as finally ending the sacerdotal sacrificial system in Jerusalem as the primary means of Jewish worship and substituted liturgy for sacrifice. Because sacrifice was permitted only in Jerusalem, diaspora Jewry had already been developing liturgy and built recollection of the sacrifices into it, with the hope of reconstructing it when Jews would again return to Jerusalem. After 70 CE, one of the tractates of the Mishnah, Yoma ("the Day"),[5] carefully preserved precisely how Yom Kippur was to be practiced at both the clerical and lay levels in anticipation of eventual rebuilding of the temple in Jerusalem.

The Western Christian tradition, on the other hand, discarded the requirement of centering sacrificial worship in Jerusalem and reconstructed the cult vicariously using a clerical structure that imitated the sacrificial rites in Jerusalem and liturgicized them. Salvation, reenacted in the mass, focused on the singular death of John's "lamb of God" (John 1:29). This verse, extensively elaborated by the theological treatise known as the Letter to the Hebrews, effectively sacerdotalized Jesus, reenvisioning the Older

---

5. Mishnah Yoma means "the Day." The fifth tractate of the second division of the Mishnah, "Appointed Times (seasons)." It details priestly practice for the Day of Atonement and proper observance of the day by the people.

Repentance and Forgiveness

Testament in terms left behind by the church's Jewish cousin in favor of the synagogue with a highly developed and democratic liturgy that endures to this day. Judaism has no priesthood. There is no liturgical function reserved for the ordained. Returning to the Christian case, on the theological side, with Augustine, sin became the preoccupation of the West, and he identified an atonement soteriology in *De Trinitate* 13. In the early Middle Ages, Anselm of Canterbury elaborated that soteriology as penal substitution to encourage fear of punishing divine wrath and guilt over sin (*Cur Deus Homo*). Penal substitutionary atonement became the quintessential expiatory means that encourages repentance and enacts divine forgiveness. It also perhaps cultivated anxiety for some, shame that reached a crisis point in the person of Martin Luther.

Once the sacrificial system was gone and the Jews were exiled from Jerusalem, they had to reconstruct atonement, repentance, and forgiveness to be portable, as Christians also did to carry its various forms of the worship of God abroad. Of the many Leviticus and Numbers texts on atonement, Jews focused on Leviticus 23:26–32:

> The Lord spoke to Moses, saying: Now, the tenth day of this seventh month is the day of atonement; it shall be a holy convocation for you: you shall deny yourselves and present the Lord's offering by fire; and you shall do no work during that entire day; for it is a day of atonement, to make atonement on your behalf before the lord your God. For anyone who does not practice self-denial during that entire day shall be cut off from the people. And anyone who does any work during that entire day, such a one I will destroy from the midst of the people. You shall do no work: it is a statute forever throughout your generations in all your settlements. It shall be to you a Sabbath of complete rest, and you shall deny yourselves; on the ninth day of the month at evening, from evening to evening you shall keep your Sabbath.

Rabbinic Judaism transformed this requirement into the penitential day of days following the instruction as carefully as possible except for the "Lord's offering by fire" that was prohibited outside Jerusalem. Yom Kippur is an annual twenty-four-hour fast from food, drink, bathing, anointing, sex, and work, as prescribed in Mishnah Yoma. Medieval Judaism liturgicized the twenty-four-hour period. Practicing Jews will go home to sleep, but will be at prayer in the synagogue for perhaps sixteen of these twenty-four hours. There is an entire prayer book (maḥzor) for this day alone, and another for the celebration of the New Year that precedes it by ten days.

The penitential season lasts thirty-eight days beginning with Ellul, the last month of the Jewish calendar. It is devoted to penitential self-reflection. Lent is its Christian counterpart. During Ellul, Psalm 27 is added to the daily prayers, along with special penitential prayers.

While classical Western Christianity distinguishes not only original sin from actual sin but also mortal from venial sin, as well as seven "deadly sins," Judaism has a different structure. Rabbinic Judaism does identify what might be called cardinal sins: murder, sexual impropriety, and idolatry. These are sins for which death atones, ameliorating the fear of death for these transgressors. A deathbed confession comparable to Christianity's last rites paves the way for repentance, forgiveness, and reconciliation that as a package yield psychological relief. Lesser sins are dealt with through prayer, alms, and repentance that complement Yom Kippur. Judaism also distinguishes sins committed maliciously from those committed out of ignorance and those committed inadvertently, recognizing greater and lesser culpability accordingly. It further differentiates sins against God from those committed against other people (m. Yoma 8d–f). "For transgressions done between man and the Omnipresent, the Day of Atonement atones. For transgressions between man and man, the Day of Atonement atones, only if the man will regain the good will of his friend."[6]

Perhaps some Jews today are considering another category: sins against the earth itself. I do not know.

The month of Ellul reaches a climax on the Saturday night before Rosh Hashanah with an annual midnight penitential service. Special prayers and readings heighten the penitential atmosphere heading into the ten days between Rosh Hashanah and Yom Kippur, the Days of Awe, the Ten Penitential Days that in turn prepare for approaching God on Yom Kippur itself. I have a British prayer book that consolidates all the penitential fasts and prayers. One hundred pages are devoted to prayers for these ten days. Here is a representative sample from a prayer on the fifth day:

> Our Father, our King, be gracious to us and answer us, for we have no (good) deeds of our own; deal charitably and kindly with us and save us. As for us, we know not what to do, but our eyes are upon you. Remember O Lord, your mercies and kindnesses, for they have been from of old. Let your kindness, O Lord, be upon us. According even as we hope for you. Retain not our former

---

6. Jacob Neusner, *Judaism: The Evidence of the Mishnah*, Brown Judaic Studies 129, 2nd ed. (Atlanta: Scholars, 1988), 279.

iniquities against us; let your compassion come speedily to meet us; for we are brought very low. Be gracious to us, O Lord, be gracious to us; for we are exceedingly sated with contempt. In wrath remember to be merciful. For he knows our nature; he remembers that we are dust. Help us. O God of our salvation, for the sake of your glorious name; and deliver us, and grant atonement for our sins, for your name's sake.[7]

During this season, Jews are encouraged to seek out anyone whom they may have wronged during the preceding year to make restitution as is possible and seek forgiveness.

Christianity, which does not distinguish sins against God from sins against other people, has nothing matching this practice; all sins are brought to the cross of Christ. Social, political, and civil insecurity are as nothing compared to the eternal salvation offered by the cross. For its part, on the horizontal plane, a rabbinic source enjoins people to seek out those whom they have offended as many as three times if necessary to allow time for reflection and reconciliation to the extent possible. Should reconciliation escape reach, the penitent is encouraged to carry the weight to God on Yom Kippur, whose gracious attribute of mercy is presumed to overpower his punishing attribute of justice in such cases.

Without a penitential system comparable to the medieval Christian structure or the sacerdotal sacramental system, Jews relied on liturgical form and recommended personal practice to weather personal crises and social impediments to their spiritual/psychological well-being.

These liturgical markers should arouse considerable self-reflection during this six-week period. Designated liturgical prayers and hymns of the season, most of them medieval in origin, include long formulaic lists of sins confessed by the whole congregation as if the entire community committed all of them. Each sin is introduced with "Our Father, our King, we have sinned against you by . . ." The signature confession of sin for the day, known by its opening words "For the sin that we have committed against you by . . ." is comparable to classical Christianity's confession of sin found in the 1979 Episcopal *Book of Common Prayer*. It is recited or set to music and repeated multiple times throughout the penitential season.

In addition to atonement for past sins, the Day of Atonement acquired the dramatic connotation of bearing the weight of the individual's destiny for the coming year based on divine judgement. The metaphorical Book

---

7. Abraham Rosenfeld, *Selichot for the Whole Year*, 4th ed. (London: Labworth, 1969).

of Life is opened during this season, and one's destiny for the coming year is inscribed. It is sealed at the end of Yom Kippur in a concluding service marking "the locking of the gates." It lasts about an hour and is prayed standing because the holy ark is open, symbolizing the open gates of God's judgment about to close. Everyone is inscribed; who will live and who will die by fire, by strangling, by drowning, by stoning, by accident. Death was ever present in a precarious world where pirates and vandals, fire and theft marauded at will. For Jews, life was particularly fragile in Christianly controlled lands. During these Ten Days of Awe, Jews greet one another with "May you be inscribed for a good year." Anxiety is stilled by the slogan "Yet prayer, repentance and almsgiving mitigate the severity of the divine decree."

Similarities That Sustain

In sum, Christianity and Judaism both took the biblical sacrificial system seriously for their understanding of repentance and forgiveness. Both have penitential seasons lasting nearly six weeks for self-examination leading up to an intense seven-to-ten-day period of dramatic liturgies that culminate in the holiest day of the liturgical year. Lenten discipline traditionally encouraged abstention from meat, sweets, and alcohol, for example, as prescribed by the medieval penitential manuals for various offenses. The penitential discipline of Ellul, by contrast, does not encourage abstaining from gastronomic pleasures in advance of Yom Kippur. Other fast days are marked throughout the liturgical year and other fasts to be observed under certain conditions (Mishnah Taanit with special penitential prayers for each).[8] Instead Ellul encourages interpersonal reconciliation reinforcing Judaism's community orientation. For its part, Christian liturgy retains a remnant of interpersonal reconciliation in the recent practice of the passing of the peace before Holy Communion, respecting Matthew 5:23–24: "So when you are offering your gift at the altar, if you remember that your brother or sister has something against you, leave your gift there before the altar and go; first be reconciled to your brother or sister, and then come and offer your gift." This text is perhaps a gloss on the Mishnah Yoma passage I

---

8. Mishna Taanit means "Fast." The ninth tractate of the second division of the Mishnah, "Appointed Times." It deals with all fasting practices of the Jewish liturgical year, as well as fasts in time of need.

read. Today Lenten fasting is being reinterpreted in interpersonal and psychological categories. One such adaptation is as follows:

> Fast from judging others; feast on Christ dwelling in them.
> Fast from fear of illness; feast on the healing power of God.
> Fast from words that pollute; feast on speech that purifies.
> Fast from discontent; feast on gratitude.
> Fast from anger; feast on patience.
> Fast from pessimism; feast on optimism.
> Fast from bitterness; feast on forgiveness.
> Fast from self-concern; feast on compassion.
> Fast from gossip; feast on purposeful silence.
> Fast from problems that overwhelm; feast on prayers that sustain.
> Fast from worry. Feast in faith.

This list echoes the lists of sins recited by the congregation in the synagogue on Yom Kippur.

In its turn, Christianity reconstructed the biblical priesthood with holy orders while Judaism abandoned it, although a remnant remains in the custom of identifying those who believe they are descended from the ancient priests and Levites and granting them priority in one aspect of the chanting of the Torah in the synagogue service.

In conclusion, although Judaism and Christianity offer different solutions to different questions, Judaism asking how best to organize society and Christianity asking how best to create humble people, both are interested in cultivating harmonious well-functioning societies. Through working from different starting points, they both prescribe repentance and offer forgiveness. Judaism and Anglicanism in particular are prayer-book communities whose liturgical life centers spiritual life on tucking people up into a venerable but ever adapting ancient heritage that plants people in community life with God in worship.

Fortunately, we live at a moment when interest in improving interfaith understanding and cooperation is strong. This can carry us beyond polite but ignorant tolerance. Indeed, there is barely a Jewish or a Christian congregation that does not have members of the other community in its midst. It behooves us all to take advantage of the opportunity to embrace our neighbors, not because it is the right thing to do, but because we need them to continue growing into our best self. I will conclude with another anecdote relevant to a Christian audience. Last fall I took a large class to the local synagogue for Sabbat morning services. I was seated next to one student already functioning as a pastor. He had been to Jewish services numerous times before with Jewish friends growing up. In the middle of the service, he leaned over and whispered in my ear: "You know, I could learn something from these people." Perhaps his words resonate. And perhaps Jewish visitors to our churches will also find riches among us to take home with them. That is not for us to determine or even to anticipate. But let us all be encouraged, trusting that the grace of God accompanies us as we bumble our way toward light and truth, hopefully in collegial friendship.

3

The Virtue of the Sacrament of Penance: A Thomist Reply to Lutheran Concerns

Dominic M. Langevin, OP

THE VERY FIRST THESIS of the Ninety-Five Theses of the young Martin Luther is, "When our Lord and Master Jesus Christ said, 'Repent (poenitentiam agite),' he willed the entire life of believers to be one of repentance."[1] A few centuries earlier, the young Thomas Aquinas wrote,

> The time for contrition is entirely the status of the present life. For as long as someone is in the midst of a journey, he detests the inconvenient things by which he is impeded or delayed in the attainment of the goal of the journey. Wherefore, since the movement of our journey toward God is delayed through past sin, in that the time that had been determined for this movement cannot be recovered . . . , it is right that always in the time of this life the state of contrition should remain with respect to the detestation of sin.[2]

---

1. *Luther's Works*, ed. Jaroslav Pelikan and Helmut T. Lehmann (Philadelphia: Muhlenberg and Fortress; St. Louis: Concordia, 1955–86), 31:25. All citations from the works of Martin Luther are from this edition unless *The Book of Concord* is referenced.

2. "Contritionis tempus est totus praesentis vitae status. Quamdiu enim aliquis est in statu viae, detestatur incommoda quibus a perventione ad terminum viae impeditur vel retardatur. Unde, cum per peccatum praeteritum viae nostrae cursus in Deum retardetur, quia tempus illud quod erat deputatum ad currendum recuperari non potest, ut supra dictum est; oportet quod semper in vitae hujus tempore status contritionis maneat quantum ad peccati detestationem" (*Scriptum super libros Sententiarum*, ed. Pierre

The beginning of Luther's Reform, now five hundred years old, and the teaching of the primary theologian of the Council of Trent have remarkably similar elements. And yet, quite distinct paths of repentance and forgiveness have been delineated by the Catholic and Evangelical communities.

In this essay, I will provide an overview of the history and theology of the Catholic sacrament of penance with an eye to ecumenical dimensions, particularly with respect to the Evangelical communion. I will treat the subject in four parts. First, I will give a historical overview of the basic theological and pastoral tensions in patristic and medieval penance. Then, I will outline the synthesis of Saint Thomas Aquinas. Third, I will explore the approach of Luther and early Lutheranism. I shall limit my treatment to the Lutheran tradition for the sake of keeping our study to a manageable length and because of the importance of Catholic-Lutheran dialogue at this time of the five-hundredth anniversary. Finally, I will return to the Thomistic idea of the virtue of penance and develop how this personal lifestyle of penance entails turning to a hierarchical intervention of the church.

I will have to be brief in so many ways and will orient the essay's focus toward the virtue of penance. I will do so for two reasons. First, the virtue undergirds the entire liturgical and sacramental practice of the penitent: his contrition, confession, and satisfaction. The Catholic community has gradually come to value this virtue. Those Catholic theologians who have not done so have instead created a warped view of the sacrament, one that emphasizes the role of the priest-confessor to the detriment of the penitent. Aspects of that flawed thinking, I dare say, are dangerously alive and well within certain sectors of the Catholic community today. Second, the virtue of penance provides a bridge to Evangelical concerns about serious, ongoing recognition of men's sinfulness and our need to implore God's mercy, that is, to Luther's call for "the entire life of believers to be one of repentance."

The language of "virtue" may strike some (e.g., certain Lutheran and Reformed Christians) as an unfortunate or evil works-based human construct.[3] That concern involves broader notions of theological anthropology

---

Mandonnet, and Marie-Fabien Moos, 4 vols. [Paris: Lethielleux, 1929–47], lib. IV, d. 17, q. 2, a. 4, qla 1, corpus; translations from the *Scriptum* are my own).

3. Concerning Luther's view of virtue, see Gilbert C. Meilaender, *The Theory and Practice of Virtue* (Notre Dame: University of Notre Dame Press, 1984), 10:105–26; Jennifer A. Herdt, "Virtue's Semblance: Erasmus and Luther on Pagan Virtue and the Christian Life," *Journal of the Society of Christian Ethics* 25 (2005) 137–62; Jennifer A. Herdt, *Putting On Virtue: The Legacy of the Splendid Vices* (Chicago: University of Chicago Press,

and soteriology, notions upon which I will try to touch. From the outset, I want to emphasize that for Aquinas, if an act of penance is good and salvific, God's grace is at the source, middle, and end of that act. Pelagianism and Semi-Pelagianism are always to be rejected. Nonetheless, I will continue to use the language of virtue out of respect to Aquinas's own system, just as I will try to respect the language of Luther. For those ill at ease with Aquinas's language, I would ask that they try to look at the underlying common threads with their own theological tradition. There is a notion of interior repentance that is shared both by Aquinas's understanding of the virtue of penance and by Luther's theology. Furthermore, as I will show at the end of this chapter, the language of virtue may have more common Catholic-Lutheran currency than sometimes supposed.

A Brief History of the Sacrament up to the Thirteenth Century

Biblical roots for the Catholic sacrament of penance or the Protestant ordinance could include—and historically have included—such texts as Christ's call to repentance at the beginning of his public ministry,[4] his bestowal of the keys to Peter,[5] his teaching on fraternal correction and corporate binding and loosing,[6] and his bestowal of this power to the Apostles as a

---

2008), 173–96; Elizabeth Agnew Cochran, "Faith, Love, and Stoic Assent: Reconsidering Virtue in the Reformed Tradition," *Journal of Moral Theology* 3 (2014) 199n2.

4. E.g., "repent, and believe in the gospel" (Mark 1:15). All Scripture citations are taken from the Revised Standard Version, Catholic Edition (1965–66).

5. "I will give you the keys of the kingdom of heaven, and whatever you bind on earth shall be bound in heaven, and whatever you loose on earth shall be loosed in heaven" (Matt 16:19).

6. "If your brother sins against you, go and tell him his fault, between you and him alone. If he listens to you, you have gained your brother. But if he does not listen, take one or two others along with you, that every word may be confirmed by the evidence of two or three witnesses. If he refuses to listen to them, tell it to the church; and if he refuses to listen even to the church, let him be to you as a Gentile and a tax collector. Truly, I say to you, whatever you bind on earth shall be bound in heaven, and whatever you loose on earth shall be loosed in heaven" (Matt 18:15–18).

Paschal blessing and injunction.[7] One thinks, too, of Saint Paul's teaching and practice of excommunication and pardon in 1 and 2 Corinthians.[8]

Beyond the biblical testimony, the organized, ritualized practice of individual penance has various historical markers.[9] One such literary witness is *The Shepherd of Hermas*, dated to the mid-second century. Hermas presents how a Christian can be forgiven after baptism. But it is possible that Hermas is unsure whether a person can be forgiven more than once after baptism. At least some in the later tradition interpreted Hermas as holding only for such one-time forgiveness. It seems that Hermas had the prudential pastoral view that it would be difficult for repeat sinners to truly be sorry for their repeated sins. This realism or pessimism—depending upon one's perspective—was hardened by certain later bishops and theologians into the notion that the ecclesial practice of postbaptismal penance could only be done once.[10] So, *The Shepherd of Hermas* is the first to enunciate two concerns that would bedevil saints and sinners through the ages: first, that insufficient personal contrition would not meet with divine forgiveness,

---

7. "Receive the Holy Spirit. If you forgive the sins of any, they are forgiven; if you retain the sins of any, they are retained" (John 20:22–23). For an overview of the biblical material on penance, see Robert L. Fastiggi, *The Sacrament of Reconciliation: An Anthropological and Scriptural Understanding* (Chicago: Hillenbrand, 2017), 20–36; Paul F. Palmer, *Sacraments of Healing and of Vocation* (Englewood Cliffs: Prentice-Hall, 1963), 1–10; Bernhard Poschmann, *Penance and the Anointing of the Sick*, trans. Francis Courtney, (Freiburg: Herder, 1964), 5–19; James Dallen, *The Reconciling Community: The Rite of Penance* (New York: Pueblo, 1986), 5–18; Jean-Philippe Revel, *La réconciliation*, Traité des sacrements 5 (Paris: Cerf, 2015), 24–130, 138–51, 159–64, 168–72, 201–14.

8. 1 Cor 5; 2 Cor 2:10.

9. The classic account of the overall history of the sacrament of penance is Poschmann, *Penance and the Anointing of the Sick*. Even after many years and many attempts to correct certain aspects, it retains its importance. Significant new contributions and surveys have been made in the following works: Dallen, *The Reconciling Community: The Rite of Penance*; Abigail Firey, ed., *A New History of Penance* (Leiden: Brill, 2008); Rob Meens, *Penance in Medieval Europe, 600–1200* (Cambridge, UK: Cambridge University Press, 2014). For specifically the patristic era, see Karl Rahner, *Penance in the Early Church*, trans. Lionel Swain, Theological Investigations 15 (New York: Crossroad, 1982); Everett Ferguson, "Early Church Penance," *Restoration Quarterly* 36 (1994) 81–100; Allan D. Fitzgerald, "Penance," in *The Oxford Handbook of Early Christian Studies*, ed. Susan Ashbrook Harvey and David G. Hunter (Oxford: Oxford University Press, 2008), 786–807. An emphasis of recent historiography has been the diversity of ways that Christians could do penance through the ages, particularly the liturgical or cultural forms for such penance. Such research would support the importance of the virtue of penance while not limiting its practice to the sacrament of penance.

10. Poschmann, *Penance and the Anointing of the Sick*, 26–35.

and second, that there could be some limit to the Church's ability to forgive sinners. The balance between harshness and leniency was variable. While some would see *The Shepherd of Hermas* as too strict, Tertullian (c. 160–c. 225), in his Montanist phase, decried it as shockingly lax. Tertullian said that this text is itself an "adulteress," that Hermas is a "prostitutor even of the Christian sacrament,"[11] and that Hermas is a "shepherd of adulterers."[12]

By the third century, we have indications of an organized system of public penance for Christians who have sinned gravely.[13] This system was called *exomologesis* (ἐξομολόγησις), coming from the verb "to confess."[14] The term was used as an accepted, traditional one in Tertullian,[15] Saint Irenaeus, and Saint Clement of Alexandria, testimony about it coming from all parts of the Mediterranean world. It developed into what was later called "canonical penance," insofar as the parameters of the system were governed

11. "Sed cederem tibi, si scriptura 'pastoris,' quae sola moechos amat, diuino instrumento meruisset incidi, si non ab omni concilio ecclesiarum, etiam uestrarum, inter apocrypha et falsa iudicaretur, adultera et ipsa et inde patrona sociorum, a qua et alias initiaris, cui ille, si forte, patrocinabitur pastor, quem in calice depingis, prostitutorem et ipsum christiani sacramenti, merito et ebrietatis idolum et moechiae asylum post calicem subsecuturae, de quo nihil libentius bibas quam ouem paenitentiae secundae" (*De pudicitia* 10, according to the following edition: Tertullian, *Opera*, Corpus Christianorum, Series Latina 1–2 [Turnhout: Brepols, 1954], 2:1280–330; the translations of Tertullian are my own).

12. "Et utique receptior apud ecclesias epistola barnabae illo apocrypho pastore moechorum" (*De pudicitia* 20).

13. Concerning the limits and possibilities for our historical understanding of penitential practices in the second century, see Christine Trevett, "'I Have Heard from Some Teachers': The Second-Century Struggle for Forgiveness and Reconciliation," in *Retribution, Repentance, and Reconciliation: Papers Read at the 2002 Summer Meeting and the 2003 Winter Meeting of the Ecclesiastical History Society*, ed. Kate Cooper and Jeremy Gregory, Studies in Church History 40 (Suffolk, UK: Boydell, 2004), 5–28. Trevett seems to be skeptical that bishops had any formal role in the practice of penance, though she seems to allow for presbyteral activity (Trevett, "I Have Heard," 18, 22.). Ferguson states, "The role of the elders in the disciplinary process is met in several passages, especially in second-century sources" (Ferguson, "Early Church Penance," 100). More generally, concerning the involvement of ecclesial leaders in the second and third centuries, see Ferguson, "Early Church Penance," 87, 89, 99–100; Poschmann, *Penance and the Anointing of the Sick*, 23–26, 33.

14. "Etymology: Greek ἐξομολόγησις < ἐξομολογεῖν , < ἐξ intensive + ὁμολογεῖν to confess" ("exomologesis," in *The Oxford English Dictionary Online*, http://www.oed.com).

15. See Tertullian's explicit discussion of *exomologesis* in *De paenitentia* 9, along with helpful distinctions concerning this material in Tertullian, *Treatises on Penance: "On Penitence"* and *"On Purity"*, trans. William P. Le Saint (Westminster: Newman, 1959), 170–72nn150–52.

by ecclesial canons, the decisions of bishops and councils. We do not know if the confession of specific sins in the earliest Christian years was done to the entire local Christian community or just to a bishop or priest. Certainly, with the confession of grave sin, the sinner entered into a publicly known period of probation and separation from full communal life. He entered the *ordo paenitentium*, the order of penitents.[16] This could last for several years. The penitent was still a member of the Christian community, indeed a practicing one, but excommunicate from full participation, for instance, from Eucharistic communion. Beyond this exclusion, penitential acts could include "'prostration in sackcloth and ashes,' neglect of cleanliness, severe fasts, protracted sighing, weeping and prayer, beseeching on bended knee the assistance of the presbyters, of 'God's beloved' (in the first place are meant the martyrs and confessors) and of all the brethren."[17] Asking for the intercessory prayers of other Christians, especially those slated for martyrdom, was a first step in a long-term phenomenon in the practice of the sacrament of penance, namely, the seeking of ways to shorten or facilitate one's penitential period through the charity of others.[18] Lastly, when the penitential period was over, the penitent was reconciled via a laying on of hands by the bishop.

Tertullian and his fellow Montanists, rigorists of the third century, wanted a purer church. Tertullian said, "The Church can forgive sin, but I will not, so that others besides may not sin."[19] Montanists started to propose that not even the church "can forgive sin." They introduced a gap between what God could forgive and what the church could forgive. Everyone agreed that God could forgive any sin that he may wish. But one cannot always know in this world what God has or has not forgiven. In contrast,

16. De Jong has critiqued the notion of an order of penitents (Mayke de Jong, "Transformations of Penance," in *Rituals of Power: From Late Antiquity to the Early Middle Ages*, ed. Frans Theuws and Janet L. Nelson (Leiden: Brill, 2000), 190–202. This should not be taken to mean, however, that a publicly identifiable group of penitents did not exist. There is too much patristic evidence of such penitents to doubt their existence as a group. Among recent scholars, see, for instance, Kevin Uhalde, "Juridical Administration in the Church and Pastoral Care in Late Antiquity," in *A New History of Penance*, ed. Abigail Firey (Leiden: Brill, 2008), 101–20. The historical uncertainty concerns, rather, the features of this order of penitents (e.g., who was included, how public or private the confession or satisfaction was).

17. Poschmann, *Penance and the Anointing of the Sick*, 44.

18. Poschmann, *Penance and the Anointing of the Sick*, 76–77.

19. "Potest ecclesia donare delictum, sed non faciam, ne et alia delinquant" (*De pudicitia* 21).

a penitent can know here and now if a bishop or priest in the flesh says, "I forgive you." The Montanist gap introduced between divine forgiveness and ecclesial forgiveness entailed whether the church on earth was capable of forgiving certain sins or of repeatedly forgiving certain sins. The allegation was that the church's capacity for forgiveness was limited, not extending beyond baptism. For Montanists looking at the postbaptismal sinner, the policy was "one strike and you're out." It was a limitation against sinners, but it was also a limitation against the church's power of the keys.

That questioning of the church's power and the quest for ecclesial holiness led to Novatianism, a movement surrounding the person of the antipope Novatian (d. 257/58). Novatianism insisted that the church is only for the sinless. It denied that the church can forgive any serious post-baptismal sin, effectively denying sacramental penance. The response from Catholic pastors was vigorous, insisting that the church can forgive any sin.[20]

This was an era when sin and repentance were taken seriously. But repentance was a difficult undertaking. Were there helps beyond the standard, limited community participation in which the penitents were still allowed? There was the phenomenon of recourse to the prayers of those slated to be executed for their Christian faith. With the growth of monasticism—white martyrdom—Saint Clement of Alexandria suggested that penitents seek the prayers and guidance of monks—indeed, any holy cleric or layman—holy brothers who could encourage and strengthen their weaker brothers in the hard work of repentance. This can be called the "therapeutic" approach.[21] It did not replace ecclesiastical or liturgical penance, but served to aid it.

After the legalization of Christianity by Constantine, the phenomenon of recidivism, repeated serious sin, grew and grew. Also, the confession of lighter sins became more frequent. The structure of canonical penance remained. But entrance into the order of penitents seemed ever more daunting. Because of the heavy penitential works involved, some serious sinners hesitated until their deathbeds to enter into the order of penitents (or, for that matter, the order of the baptized). As an alternative, it was even seen as an acceptable but easier penance for a man to become a cleric or for

---

20. See the texts reprinted in Paul F. Palmer, ed., *Sacraments and Forgiveness: History and Doctrinal Development of Penance, Extreme Unction and Indulgences* (Westminster: Newman, 1959), 51–59.

21. Poschmann, *Penance and the Anointing of the Sick*, 65–66, 99–100.

anyone to enter religious life.[22] The church's recruitment of new ministers and religious vocations never looked better!

In fact, the Christian living of repentance was developing beyond the canonical system of the patristic age. From the sixth century on, the penitential system of the Celts and Anglo-Saxons grew in popularity.[23] By this point certainly, both canonical penance and Celtic penance involved private confession to a priest. But Celtic penance did not involve a publicly identifiable order of penitents. This is not to say that the prescribed penances were always invisible. But a bystander would have to ask the Christian doing difficult actions why he was acting in this (unusual) manner. Further, these penances, difficult as they were, were lighter than canonical penances. Finally, the penances were determined according to tariffs: a particular sin deserved a particular, proportionate penance. These tariffs were suggested in penitential books, "the penitentials," whose authority derived from the holiness of their authors, often monks or clerics, guided by the local bishop. Compared to the canonical system, the sacrament of penance in the Celtic system was still well-organized. But it involved a more personal character, both for the penitent and for the priest-confessor, the latter of whom individually judged the cases, determined which competing penitential book to follow, and encouraged the penitent as a therapeutic guide.

In this movement toward privatization within an ecclesial system—I say "system" because the sacrament of penance was never a totally private affair, there always being episcopal and ecclesiastical involvement—an important development occurred with respect to the timing of absolution or reconciliation. Originally, this transpired after the confession of sins and the penitential satisfaction were done. In the century before the year 1000, the order was changed. Confession came first, then absolution, then satisfaction.[24]

---

22. Poschmann, *Penance and the Anointing of the Sick*, 123.

23. Further treatment of medieval developments can be found in de Jong, "Transformations of Penance," 185–224; Sarah Hamilton, *The Practice of Penance, 900–1050* (Woodbridge, Suffolk, UK: Boydell, 2001); Firey, ed., *A New History of Penance*; Meens, *Penance in Medieval Europe, 600–1200*. Concerning recent historiography about late patristic and medieval trends toward more private celebrations of the sacrament, I find particularly cogent the questions and concerns of Thomas Tentler in his review of *The Practice of Penance, 900–1050*, by Sarah Hamilton, *The Medieval Review* 02.07.19 (2002), https://scholarworks.iu.edu/journals/index.php/tmr/article/view/15252/21370.

24. Hamilton, *Practice of Penance, 900–1050*, 143, 153, 166.

That ritual change led to a theological question: if absolution can be given immediately after confession, does this mean that a simple pronunciation of past misdeeds equals the sacrament of penance and the forgiveness of one's sins? Peter Abelard did not give a simplistic "yes" answer, but he insisted upon the penitent's contrition as the only necessary action. Contrition effected forgiveness, at least with respect to sin's eternal punishment. The church's role and the priest's role, Abelard said, were only practical, assigning satisfactory penances for the bodily, temporal punishments due to sin. The priest could also contribute prayers, but these were only efficacious if the priest were holy. As for Abelard's theories about the sacrament of penance, Saint Bernard of Clairvaux and the Synod of Sens condemned them. But one can see why they would be theologically appealing. How so? Because it is, indeed, true that contrition is the result of the grace of conversion. Abelard was a good anti-Pelagian. He was not, though, a good ecclesiastic. Against Abelard's penitential system, the Victorine School (Hugh of St. Victor and Richard of St. Victor) insisted that forgiveness occurs through the church's role, through the priest's liturgical rite of absolution.[25]

The Synthesis of Saint Thomas Aquinas

Thomas Aquinas was a great synthesizer, including with respect to the sacrament of penance and its theological history. But before looking at his theology of penance, we should take notice of his understanding of justification in general.[26] Thomas explains that justification begins with a movement of God, who infuses grace into the sinner. This grace turns the sinner toward God, so that the sinner, if he freely chooses to cooperate, can behold God, who is all true and good, and choose God. There is always a human choice, for in this life, God does not reveal himself fully but only darkly, as in a mirror. But if the human will cooperates with God's movement of converting grace, the human being can see sin as the corruption and evil that it truly is. The human being can therefore move away from sin. This human rejection of sin is matched by God's remission of sin. So,

---

25. Poschmann, *Penance and the Anointing of the Sick*, 156–62; Paul Anciaux, *La théologie du sacrement de pénitence au XIIe siècle* (Louvain: Nauwelaerts, 1949).

26. *Summa theologiae*, I-II, q. 113, focusing on a. 8. Texts from the *Summa theologiae* (*ST*) will be cited according to the corrected Leonine edition of *Summa theologiae*, 3rd ed. (Turin: San Paolo, 1999). English translations will be my own.

in Aquinas's theory of justification, the divine initiative of converting grace moves man, who is left free to cooperate in his transformation.

The sacrament of penance for Aquinas is a means of this jointly divine and human mode of transformation. There are a couple of distinctive features that I will point out about Aquinas's theology of sacramental penance. First, Aquinas links the sacrament with a virtue, the virtue of penance.[27] When Aquinas writes his *Summa theologiae*, he treats all of the virtues as a block—a very long block—in his treatise on moral theology, the *Secunda pars*. The one exception is the virtue of penance, which gets placed near the beginning of his treatment on the sacrament of penance.

The virtue of penance is "a moderated sorrow for past sins with the intention of removing them."[28] The penitent moves toward "removing the result [of the past sin], namely, the hatred of God and the guilt of punishment."[29] This is sorrow with an edge against that past sin. Thomas says that the virtue of penance is a virtue of justice, for sin is an offense against what is owed to God.[30] But it is not a perfect justice, because there is not equality between God and the creature. There is, nonetheless, a connection to the theological virtues, the virtues that have God as their proper object. Thomas says that the virtue of "penance exists with faith in the passion of Christ, through which we are justified from our sins; and with the hope of forgiveness; and with the hatred of vices, which pertains

---

27. Aquinas's account of the virtue of penance has not received much sustained examination by sacramental theologians in recent times. For instance, a recent monograph (admirable in many respects) on Aquinas's theology of the sacrament gives no sustained treatment on the virtue of penance: Eric Luijten, *Sacramental Forgiveness as a Gift of God: Thomas Aquinas on the Sacrament of Penance* (Leuven: Peeters, 2003). Exceptions to this contemporary silence are Maria C. Morrow, "Reconnecting Sacrament and Virtue: Penance in Thomas's *Summa Theologiae*," *New Blackfriars* 91 (2010) 304–20; Jörgen Vijgen, "St. Thomas Aquinas and the Virtuousness of Penance: On the Importance of Aristotle for Catholic Theology," *Nova et Vetera, English Edition* 13 (2015) 601–16. Study of this virtue was a standard feature, however, of an older, Scholastic mode of sacramental theology; e.g., Dominic M. Prümmer, *Manuale theologiae moralis secundum principia S. Thomae Aquinatis*, ed. Engelbert M. Münch, 8th ed., 3 vols. (Freiburg: Herder, 1935–36), 3:220–24; Emmanuel Doronzo, *De poenitentia*, 4 vols. (Milwaukee: Bruce, 1949–53), 1:260–517; Paul Galtier, *De paenitentia: Tractatus dogmatico-historicus* (Rome: Pontificia Università Gregoriana, 1957), 9–31.

28. *ST*, III, q. 85, a. 1.

29. *ST*, III, q. 85, a. 1, ad 3.

30. *ST*, III, q. 85, a. 3.

to charity."[31] Thomas describes two corollaries to the sorrow of penance.[32] First, the penitent ceases the sin. Second, he seeks to give "recompense" for the past sin. So, with the virtue of penance, a sinner moves from internal sorrow to externalized sorrow, that is, to actions that redress the past sin and satisfy in Christ's satisfaction for the injury of that past sin.

The virtue of penance can take a number of forms. One is the sacrament of penance, for which the virtue acts as a foundation or "principle" for the entire sacramental process.[33] That process for Aquinas is described in a tripartite structure.[34] A kind of sacred temporality moves from (1) the exterior, liturgical sign (the *sacramentum tantum*) to (2) the combined intermediate effect and causative sign (the *res et sacramentum*) all the way to (3) the effected grace (the *res tantum*). In the exterior sign of step 1, the penitent, acting according to the virtue of penance, offers a kind of matter for the liturgical sacrament. That analogous matter is threefold: interior contrition, the confession of individual sins to a priest, and the performance of a satisfactory deed or deeds enjoined by the priest. The base is the interior contrition. Peter Abelard had focused upon this aspect. Aquinas expands upon Abelard's insight by holding that the priest's role is also essential. This integrates the Victorine School and the general pastoral practice of the church. The priest's absolution is the form for the penitent's matter. The two roles, penitents and priests, come together in a concelebration. Aquinas speaks of the two working as a single act.[35] The penitent possesses the initiative. "The repenting sinner, through those things that he does and says, signifies that his heart has withdrawn from sin."[36] How could the penitent have already "withdrawn from sin"? Because of the initial grace of conversion, as specified in Aquinas's schema of justification. To this is liturgically added the priest's role. Aquinas says, "The priest, by those things that he

---

31. *ST*, III, q. 85, a. 3, ad 4.

32. *ST*, III, q. 85, a. 3.

33. *ST*, III, q. 85, a. 1, ad 1.

34. For a recent explanation and defense of the Thomistic tripartite structure of the sacrament of penance, see Gilles Emery, "Reconciliation with the Church and Interior Penance: The Contribution of Thomas Aquinas on the Question of the *Res et Sacramentum* of Penance," trans. Robert E. Williams, *Nova et Vetera*, English Edition 1 (2003) 283-301, esp. 292-97 and 300-301.

35. "In penance, there is something that is the *sacramentum tantum*, namely, the act [NB: singular] exercised as much by the repenting sinner as also by the absolving priest" (*ST*, III, q. 84, a. 1, ad 3).

36. *ST*, III, q. 84, a. 1.

does and says concerning the penitent, signifies the work of the God who is remitting sin."[37] How can God have "withdrawn [the penitent] from sin" but also be "remitting sin" through the priest? We have a perfective chain of sacramental causality whereby saving grace is communicated from God to the sinner. But the chain works in a complex fashion.[38] We can think of it as a movement from two directions. God is working bottom-up in the life of the penitent. God is working top-down via the priest.

This joint sacramental causality in the *sacramentum tantum* is a springboard to the *res et sacramentum*. If the penitent's contrition has been in some way imperfect (attrition), the liturgical rite deepens it and convicts the sinner that he should be and is sorry for his sins. This is the intermediate effect of the entire sacramental rite.

But that *res et sacramentum* is itself a springboard to another effect, the final one, the *res tantum*, which is the grace of forgiveness for the penitent. With this forgiveness of sins, there is reconciliation to God and then reconciliation with the Church.

The whole tripartite structure is a dynamic process, a stepladder from the depths of sin to a higher level of holiness, some state of sanctifying grace. And in that dynamism, the effects are cumulative. The *sacramentum tantum* moves the penitent to the state of the *res et sacramentum*, which, together with the *sacramentum tantum*, moves the penitent to the *res tantum*. And at the foundation, pushing all the way through, is the virtue of penance. The virtue animates the penitent to sacramentally cooperate with God's converting grace in order to realize the gift of forgiveness.

Luther and Early Lutheranism

Over the course of five hundred years and still today, there are a variety of Protestant approaches to a sacrament, ordinance, or ecclesial practice of penance or reconciliation.[39] There have been and are non-Catholic pastors and laity who perform a ritual that more or less approximates or tries to do what Catholics do in the sacrament of penance. For instance, certain

---

37. *ST*, III, q. 84, a. 1.

38. For a recent monograph on Thomistic sacramental causality, see Reginald Lynch, *The Cleansing of the Heart: The Sacraments as Instrumental Causes in the Thomistic Tradition* (Washington, DC: Catholic University of America Press, 2017).

39. For a general background, see James F. White, *The Sacraments in Protestant Practice and Faith* (Nashville: Abingdon, 1999), 119–25.

Repentance and Forgiveness

Anglicans or Episcopalians utilize a commonly called sacramental rite of individual reconciliation.[40] There are also Lutheran pastors who perform "individual and personal Confession and Absolution."[41] The language sometimes seems to imply a theology of direct, instrumental sacramental causality, something akin to a Roman Catholic understanding. My sense is that certain pastors nowadays are reviving these penitential practices without the largest bodies of a community (e.g., a particular synod or denomination) taking a firm theological stance on the meaning of these practices (i.e., something akin to the Augsburg Confession's articles on confession). Historically, however, the theology and practice of penance have been matters that demanded comment from the most important leaders. Martin Luther was among those who so spoke.[42]

---

40. See the various forms for "the Reconciliation of a Penitent" in the 1979 Book of Common Prayer of the Episcopal Church, with the distinction between the "absolution" given by a bishop or priest and the "declaration of forgiveness" given by a deacon or layman (*The Book of Common Prayer . . . According to the Use of the Episcopal Church* [New York: Church Hymnal Corporation, 1979], 446–52, 861). Helpful here are the historical and theological explanations provided by Marion J. Hatchett, *Commentary on the American Prayer Book* (New York: Seabury, 1981), 448–58. Of interest is the fact that an absolution formula for individual penitents has been recently revived and, indeed, with the possibility for a more indicative (as opposed to deprecatory) style. See also the injunctions to use "the sacrament of reconciliation" by various Anglo-Catholic groups such as the Society of the Holy Cross (http://www.sscamericas.org/resources/rule.html) and the Society of Catholic Priests (https://www.thescp.org/ruleoflife).

41. E.g., the Society of the Holy Trinity, noting especially chapter 5 of its 1997 "Rule" of life, which details the society's understanding and practice of confession and absolution (http://www.societyholytrinity.org/therule.html). One notes that the term "sacramental rite" is utilized but not "sacrament." The "sacramental rite" is "used . . . for the sake of the absolution, which is the word of forgiveness spoken by a fellow pastor as from God himself."

42. Concerning Luther's theology of the sacrament of penance, see E. Gordon Rupp, "Luther's Ninety-Five Theses and the Theology of the Cross," in *Luther for an Ecumenical Age: Essays in Commemoration of the 450th Anniversary of the Reformation*, ed. Carl S. Meyer (St. Louis: Concordia, 1967), 72–78; Beverley Anne Nitschke, "The Third Sacrament?: Confession and Forgiveness in the *Lutheran Book of Worship*" (PhD diss., University of Notre Dame, 1988), 144–211, UMI 8819605; David Bagchi, "Luther and the Sacramentality of Penance," in *Retribution, Repentance, and Reconciliation: Papers Read at the 2002 Summer Meeting and the 2003 Winter Meeting of the Ecclesiastical History Society*, ed. Kate Cooper and Jeremy Gregory, Studies in Church History 40 (Suffolk, UK: Boydell, 2004), 119–27; Ronald K. Rittgers, "Embracing the 'True Relic' of Christ: Suffering, Penance, and Private Confession in the Thought of Martin Luther," in *A New History of Penance*, ed. Abigail Firey (Leiden: Brill, 2008), 377–93.

It is commonly said that Luther's initial call to reform focused upon abuses with the system of indulgences.[43] However, as our opening quotation from the Ninety-Five Theses indicated, Luther's deeper concern was that interior repentance be sincere and fruitful.[44] We thus could stress the commonalities with the Catholic tradition. But that would be much too easy and simplistic. For, despite that opening quotation from the first thesis, the second thesis puts us on warning that Luther and Catholicism will not be so easily reconciled. The second thesis states, "This word ['repent'] cannot be understood as referring to the sacrament of penance, that is, confession and satisfaction, as administered by the clergy."[45] That rather profoundly challenges the Catholic sacrament of penance. Nonetheless, Luther does not reject the sacrament of penance at this time, for the next twelve or so theses are concerned with the right practice of the sacrament of penance. And the subsequent theses about Purgatory and indulgences are similarly concerned with the sinful Christian's repentance and salvation.

From the language and concepts of the Ninety-Five Theses, the early Luther can be rightly interpreted as continuing earlier medieval disputations concerning how individual human repentance cooperates with divine and ecclesial forgiveness. And even for that seemingly radical, anti-Catholic second thesis, Luther's explanation of it indicates that he is merely adopting a distinction that is not so radical, namely, the distinction between ongoing interior penance and periodic sacramental penance. Luther wrote,

> sacramental penance is temporal and cannot be done all the time; otherwise one would have to speak with the priest continually and do nothing else but confess one's sins and perform the satisfaction which has been imposed. Therefore sacramental penance cannot

---

43. E.g., White, *Sacraments in Protestant Practice and Faith*, 121.

44. Nitschke, "Third Sacrament?," 144–45. The last few decades have seen the publication of several interesting monographs on the sacrament of penance just before, during, and after the Lutheran Reformation: Thomas N. Tentler, *Sin and Confession on the Eve of the Reformation* (Princeton: Princeton University Press, 1977); W. David Myers, *"Poor, Sinning Folk": Confession and Conscience in Counter-Reformation Germany* (Ithaca: Cornell University Press, 1996); Susan C. Karant-Nunn, *The Reformation of Ritual: An Interpretation of Early Modern Germany* (London: Routledge, 1997); Katharine Jackson Lualdi and Anne T. Thayer, eds., *Penitence in the Age of Reformations* (Aldershot: Ashgate, 2000); Anne T. Thayer, *Penitence, Preaching and the Coming of the Reformation* (Aldershot: Ashgate, 2002); Ronald K. Rittgers, *The Reformation of the Keys: Confession, Conscience, and Authority in Sixteenth-Century Germany* (Cambridge: Harvard University Press, 2004).

45. *Luther's Works*, 31:25.

be the cross which Christ bids us bear [Matt. 16:24]; nor is it a mortification of the passions of the flesh.[46]

Aquinas wrote something similar:

> To repent is said in two ways, namely, according to the act and according to the habit. As for the act, it is indeed impossible for man continually to repent, for it is necessary that the act of the penitent, whether interior or exterior, be interrupted, at least by sleep and other things that pertain to the necessity of the body.
>
> In the other way, to repent is said according to the habit. And in this way, it is right that man should continually repent. This is true both insofar as man should never do anything contrary to penance by which the habitual disposition of the penitent would be ruined, and insofar as he ought in his intention to carry himself such that his past sins are always displeasing to him.[47]

The Luther of the Ninety-Five Theses had qualms about how the sacrament of penance was being lived and used the categories of medieval theology to make certain distinctions and to emphasize the priority of interior repentance.

Luther's views on the sacrament, however, evolved into a more extensive criticism, one that led him to a more fundamental rejection of the Catholic understanding and practice of the sacrament. Luther's stance is not as systematic or consistent as a twenty-first-century observer may desire, but a certain number of points can be mentioned.

Luther continued and deepened his initial pastoral sense in the Ninety-Five Theses that men were forgetting the necessity of continual interior penance. Without this, the external practices of the confession of individual sins and the sacrificial deeds of atonement (i.e., the satisfactory works) were shorn of their meaning. Indeed, it seems that Luther's view of the Catholic or "papist" practice of the sacrament of penance focused precisely on the confession of individual sins and the satisfactory penance undertaken by the penitent. Luther could acknowledge that three elements—contrition, confession, and satisfaction—are all required for the Catholic sacrament. But practically, the Catholic sacrament for Luther had come to mean just

---

46. *Explanations of the Ninety-Five Theses*, in *Luther's Works*, 31:85.

47. *ST*, III, q. 84, a. 9. See also article 8, wherein Aquinas distinguished between "internal penance," which "ought to endure until the end of life," and "external penance," which entails the acts of sacramental penance and which only "should endure up to a determined time according to the measure of the sin."

two elements: confession and satisfaction. As for the individual confession of sins, the Augsburg Confession was explicit that there was no biblically proven dominical institution of this sacramental element and that therefore it could not be required of sinners.[48] The same critique would have applied to sacramental satisfaction, although I find no direct contradiction of its dominical institution. In contrast to confession and satisfaction, then, Luther identified the evangelical sacrament with contrition and faith, both of which he finds missing among the Catholics.

In identifying the Catholic sacrament only with the external acts of confession and satisfaction, Luther critiqued the practice as Pelagian, something positively destructive of the Christian spiritual life. Herein, Luther set himself against the nominalist semi-Pelagianism of the late medieval era, a semi-Pelagianism that held that the sinner could eliminate, by his natural powers, "obstacles" to his own justification and salvation. The sinner could thereby prepare himself for the gift of grace.[49] Furthermore, Luther took the grave sinner who practiced the sacrament of penance to be attempting to merit his own salvation, which seemed nonsensical.[50] For how could any grave sinner, someone who had removed himself from the state of grace through his sin, do a graced action, a godly action, a meritorious action?

Indeed, Luther evolved a more extreme judgment of man's sinfulness. "Total depravity" may be too strong a translation or may need to be understood with various qualifications, but certainly Luther's sense of the wound or corruption of the human person was such that real, profound, lasting human improvement was not possible. Integral here is the move away from a sort of intrinsic justification to a forensic and extrinsic one. Alister McGrath, a historian of justification, wrote,

> The notional distinction, necessitated by a forensic understanding of justification, between the external act of God in pronouncing sentence, and the internal process of regeneration, along with the associated insistence upon the alien and external nature of justifying righteousness, must be considered to be the most reliable *historical* characterisation of Protestant doctrines of justification.[51]

48. Article XXV (Theodore G. Tappert, ed., *The Book of Concord: The Confessions of the Evangelical Lutheran Church*, trans. Theodore G. Tappert [Philadelphia: Fortress, 1959], 61–63).

49. Nitschke, "Third Sacrament?," 152n15.

50. Nitschke, "Third Sacrament?," 151–52.

51. Alister E. McGrath, *Iustitia Dei: A History of the Christian Doctrine of Justification*, 3rd ed. (Cambridge: Cambridge University Press, 2005), 209–10.

Repentance and Forgiveness

If it is the case that man is always a sinner even if justified (*simul iustus et peccator*), then the traditional, Catholic promise of the sacrament of penance—namely, the promise that the forgiveness of sins and growth in holiness are possible through a specific, liturgical course of action—is illusory. Even more so if the Christian is not just *simul iustus et peccator* but also *semper peccator, semper penitens, sempus iustus* (always a sinner, always doing penance, always just).[52] Thus, it would be a waste of time for the Christian—even the proverbial holy, old grandmother in the pews—to enumerate actual sins in a sacramental confession. The depth of sin—powered by the *peccatum radicale*, the root sin[53]—is too great.[54]

With respect to the absolution traditionally offered by a priest, Luther denied the absolute need for a priest. He thought that it was preferable for a priest or pastor to give the word of forgiveness, but a layperson would suffice if needed.[55] De facto, Luther herein returned to the patristic therapeutic, accompaniment model. Aquinas had said that confession to a layman was salutary when absolutely no priest was available, although the interchange was not a sacrament. It was Scotus who first denied absolutely any emergency confession to a layman.[56] By Luther's time, holding for lay confession was not an accepted option. Luther adopted it though.

The Apology of the Augsburg Confession also denied the judicial quality of the absolution:

> When someone objects that a judge must hear a case before pronouncing sentence, that is irrelevant because the ministry of absolution is in the area of blessing or grace, not of judgment or law. The ministers of the church therefore have the command to forgive sins; they do not have the command to investigate secret sins.[57]

The priest would also not assign a satisfactory penance to a penitent. For Lutheranism, "binding and loosing" became just loosing.

---

52. McGrath, *Iustitia Dei*, 226.

53. Eberhard Jüngel, *Justification: The Heart of the Christian Faith*, trans. Jeffrey F. Cayzer (London: Bloomsbury, 2001), 125.

54. Nitschke, "Third Sacrament?," 153–57.

55. Nitschke, "Third Sacrament?," 172n60.

56. Poschmann, *Penance and the Anointing of the Sick*, 188.

57. Article XII (Tappert, *Book of Concord*, 197). See Nitschke, "Third Sacrament?," 166–67.

As for the absolution given by a Lutheran pastor, it is difficult to determine the efficacy of that absolution. Is it causative of forgiveness in an instrumental fashion? In the 1529 "Short Order of Confession before the Priest for the Common Man," Luther does not have any true formula of absolution. The penitent does say to the priest, "I . . . ask that you, in God's stead, would declare unto me my sins forgiven and comfort me with the word of God."[58] So, the priest's role here would seem to depart from the traditional understanding of binding and loosing. Alternately, in the 1531 edition of the *Small Catechism*, Luther had a more expansive role for the priest. Here, Luther wrote that the penitent "[receives] absolution or forgiveness from the confessor as from God himself, by no means doubting but firmly believing that [his] sins are thereby forgiven before God in heaven."[59] A bit later, the penitent is instructed to "say to the confessor: 'Dear Pastor, please hear my confession and declare that my sins are forgiven for God's sake.'"[60] In response, for the absolution portion, the confessor asks, "Do you believe that the forgiveness I declare is the forgiveness of God?" Then he gives the absolution, "Be it done for you as you have believed. According to the command of our Lord Jesus Christ, I forgive you your sins in the name of the Father and of the Son and of the Holy Spirit. Amen. Go in peace."[61] So, there are elements that are suggestive of a more directly forgiving role for the priest or pastor. In this respect, in the *Large Catechism*, Luther explains that the absolution "is a work which God does, when he absolves me of my

---

58. *Luther's Works*, 53:117.
59. "Confession and Absolution," in Tappert, *Book of Concord*, 349–50.
60. Tappert, *Book of Concord*, 350.
61. Tappert, *Book of Concord*, 351. Unfortunately, this portion of the *Small Catechism* was only drafted in German ("Und ich, aus dem Befehl unsers Herrn Jesu Christi, vergebe dir deine Sünden im Namen des Vaters und des Sohnes und des Heiligen Geistes. Amen," as edited in *D. Martin Luthers Werke: Kritische Gesamtausgabe* [Weimar: Hermann Böhlaus Nachfolger, 1883–2009], 30/2:387), so it is unclear whether Luther would have used the same formula in Latin as was typical at that time for the sacrament of penance ("Ego te absolvo a peccatis tuis, in nomine Patris, et Filii, et Spiritus Sancti"). It is notable that the official 1584 Latin edition of the Book of Concord chose an alternate expression, "Et ego ex mandato Domini nostri Iesu Christi remitto tibi tua peccata in nomine Patris, Filii et Spiritus Sancti. Amen" (*Concordia Triglotta: The Symbolical Books of the Ev. Lutheran Church, German-Latin-English*, ed. F. Bente [St. Louis: Concordia, 1921], 554). From a Catholic perspective, this alternate Latin phrasing would not be an impediment to a "perfected sacrament." See Luther's Catholic interlocutor, Cardinal Cajetan, on this subject: Thomas de Vio Cajetan, *In Summa theologiae*, in Thomas Aquinas, *Opera omnia iussu impensaque Leonis XIII P. M.* (Rome: Propaganda Fide, 1888–1906), III, q. 84, a. 3, page 12:290.

sins through a word placed in the mouth of a man."[62] And there are elements that are suggestive of a more simply declarative role. It would seem that the declarative, non-instrumental quality is more likely. Certainly, later Lutheranism took this view.[63]

So, Luther and early Lutheranism entailed many important departures from Catholic doctrine and practice with respect to the sacrament of penance. All the same, Luther encouraged confession as necessary for each Christian. He desired that the priest or pastor declare or give an absolution to the sinner. His "Brief Exhortation to Confession" in the *Large Catechism* has some powerful exhortations indeed (although not always politically correct ones, for the pope is called "God's devil and hangman" and lazy, non-confessing Christians are called "pigs"!).[64] Luther writes to the sinner in praise of Evangelical confession,

> If you are poor and miserable, then go and make use of the healing medicine. He who feels his misery and need will develop such a desire for confession that he will run toward it with joy. But those who ignore it and do not come of their own accord, we let go their way. However, they ought to know that we do not regard them as Christians.[65]

A good Christian wants confession; someone who does not is "no Christian" and "[despises] the Gospel."[66] Indeed, Luther says, "If you are a Christian, you should be glad to run more than a hundred miles for confession, not under compulsion but rather coming and compelling us to offer it."[67] Any zealous Catholic priest would say the same. But, some of Luther's lines that seem like brilliant gems to Catholic ears perhaps seemed like dark coal to other Lutheran ears, those who found them too Catholic. It may be no surprise, then, that this "section on confession . . . was omitted in

---

62. "A Brief Exhortation to Confession," in Tappert, *Book of Concord*, 459.

63. Nitschke, "Third Sacrament?," 186–87, 196.

64. Tappert, *Book of Concord*, 457–61. See Nitschke, "Third Sacrament?," 172–73: "Confession and absolution, rather than being something indifferent or foreign to the Christian life, is, in fact, the real thing about Christian existence. Renewal in baptismal piety or spirituality entails recovery of the practice of confession/absolution."

65. Tappert, *Book of Concord*, 460.

66. Tappert, *Book of Concord*, 460.

67. Tappert, *Book of Concord*, 460.

the [sixteenth-century] Jena edition of Luther's Works and in the German Book of Concord, hence also in several later editions of the Catechism."[68]

Indeed, the final results are mixed. "Luther's theology of penance reveals a certain inconsistency and ambiguity—on the one hand, confession/absolution is claimed to be of great value; on the other, it is laid aside as something of little significance."[69] The sacrament of penance was reshaped by larger questions of justification. Practically speaking, the allowance of general, vague confession (for instance, during the celebration of the Lord's Supper) indirectly killed off individual, specific confession.[70] As Luther sensed and warned against in his "Brief Exhortation to Confession" in the *Large Catechism*, Evangelical freedom could lead to effective disuse[71] or theological rejection.

The Catholic response to Luther with respect to the sacrament of penance occurred on two planes. First, the distorted views among the clergy and laity, as well as the distorted theories in the theological faculties that supported or countenanced the distorted pastoral practices, had to be corrected by the Council of Trent. In many theological respects, the Council of Trent rejected the nominalistic and late Scholastic approaches that were current in the theological faculties in the fifteen and early sixteenth centuries. Instead, it went back to the Thomistic synthesis that had been enunciated by the Magisterium since the Councils of Constance in the 1410s[72] and Florence in the 1430s.[73] It emphasized the unity of penance with the grace of justification, and the unity of the penitent's contrition, confession, and satisfaction with the priest's absolution. In 1551, the Council of Trent dedicated a Decree on the Sacrament of Penance in its fourteenth session. But already in its sixth session, in 1547, the Council spelled out how

---

68. Tappert, *Book of Concord*, 457n6.

69. Nitschke, "Third Sacrament?," 204.

70. Nitschke, "Third Sacrament?," 174–98, especially 198.

71. Nitschke, "Third Sacrament?," 205. But, for countertestimony concerning the practice of the rite of penance in post-Luther Lutheranism, see Rittgers, "Embracing the 'True Relic' of Christ," 392–93.

72. See especially paragraphs 1157, 1260–61, 1263, and 1265 in Heinrich Denzinger et al., eds., *Compendium of Creeds, Definitions, and Declarations on Matters of Father and Morals* (San Francisco: Ignatius, 2012). This *Compendium* will hereafter be abbreviated as *DH*.

73. See *DH* 1323.

justification could occur for the baptized Christian through the sacrament of penance.[74]

As a second response to the Reformation and as a complement to the theological course set by the Council of Trent, there was a Catholic renaissance in the living of the sacrament of penance. Notable here is Saint Charles Borromeo, cardinal archbishop of Milan.[75] Under his oversight, there was the invention of confessional boxes in order to aid sacramental secrecy. There was also the birth of the post-Tridentine seminary system in order to train men as holy, wise priests capable of confessional practice rooted in the conciliar theology, men who could not be the easy targets of Protestant critique.

The Verticality of the Virtue of Penance

Enriched by the history of the sacrament of penance, let us return to the virtue of penance and explore a sacramental-moral question. Comparing the penitent and the priest-confessor in the sacrament of penance, the priest could be identified as part of the church's hierarchy and thus as somehow higher than the penitent. He could be seen as representing the vertical. By contrast, the penitent could be characterized as the horizontal, especially if we think of the penitent's virtue of penance as a horizontal foundation for the tripartite, progressive dynamism of the Thomistic sacrament of penance. This analogy of horizontal and vertical is not perfect. In a certain respect, this image clashes with my earlier analysis of the top-down and the bottom-up chain of sacramental causality. But, now, with this last

---

74. See *DH* 1542–43, especially the following: "Hence it must be taught that the repentance of a Christian after his fall into sin differs vastly from repentance at the time of baptism. It includes not only giving up sins and detesting them, or 'a broken and contrite heart' [Ps 51:17], but also their sacramental confession, or at least the desire to confess them when a suitable occasion will be found, and the absolution of a priest; it also includes satisfaction by fasts, almsgiving, prayer, and other pious exercises of the spiritual life, not indeed for the eternal punishment that, together with the guilt, is remitted by the reception or the desire of the sacrament, but for the temporal punishment, which, as Sacred Scripture teaches, is not always entirely remitted, as is done in baptism, to those who, ungrateful to the grace of God they have received, have grieved the Holy Spirit [cf. Eph 4:30] and have not feared to violate the temple of God [cf. 1 Cor 3:17]."

75. Wietse de Boer, *The Conquest of the Soul: Confession, Discipline, and Public Order in Counter-Reformation Milan* (Leiden: Brill, 2001); Wietse de Boer, "At Heresy's Door: Borromeo, Penance, and Confessional Boundaries in Early Modern Europe," in *A New History of Penance*, ed. Abigail Firey (Leiden: Brill, 2008), 343–75.

image of the horizontal and the vertical, I would like to investigate whether the horizontal virtue of penance implies a verticality, an outreach to other human beings, indeed, an outreach to the ecclesial hierarchy.

Speaking in the abstract, the repentance of the sinner could remain at the level of the individual sinner with no other human persons involved. Such repentance could even be caused by God. But that would not be a Catholic understanding of repentance. Thomas's virtue of penance can help us to see the richer, more human possibilities for repentance. As mentioned earlier, for Aquinas, a corollary of the virtue of penance is the voluntary desire to redress the wrong. What are the contours of that desire to redress the wrong?

When Aquinas discusses the virtue of penance, he gives a more elaborate explanation of justification beyond the fourfold movement of justification in general. He gives a sixfold movement.[76] This is the justification of a baptized sinner. It is similar to what the Council of Trent would describe.[77] Aquinas's sixfold justification involves a process whereby God uses the gifts that he has already given in baptism. The process ends with charity and filial fear moving the sinner to "voluntarily [offer] amends to God."

To whom should "amends" be made? All sin has a communal dimension. It offends our communion with God and with all other persons, angelic and human. There is no such thing as a private sin, even if done in the privacy of one's bedroom or the privacy of one's mind. All repentance must counter the social wounds of sin via a communal act of contrition and satisfaction.[78] The virtue of penance, moved by God's "movement of charity," would incline one to an expansive response. If the priest is the icon and instrument and intercessor with Christ—and Catholicism holds that he is—and if the priest is the icon and instrument and intercessor with the church—Catholicism holds for that too—then the virtuous penitent is

---

76. ST, III, q. 85, a. 5, gives the following schema: (1) "the operation of God converting the heart," (2) "a movement of faith," (3) "a movement of servile fear whereby someone is withdrawn from his sins by the fear of punishments," (4) "a movement of hope by which someone, under the hope of the pardon to be obtained, assumes the intention of amending," (5) "a movement of charity by which sin is displeasing to someone in itself and no longer due to its punishments," and (6) "a movement of filial fear by which, due to a reverence for God, someone voluntarily offers amends to God."

77. DH 1542–43.

78. I write "satisfaction" here intentionally. Even though the details of the act of sacramental satisfaction are often unknown to anyone beyond the priest-confessor and the penitent, that satisfaction per se has a communal dimension, for it heals and builds up the community wounded by sin.

Repentance and Forgiveness

going to be expansive and to reach high and broad to express his sorrow. This is the expansiveness of Zacchaeus: "Behold, Lord, the half of my goods I give to the poor; and if I have defrauded any one of anything, I restore it fourfold."[79]

A related but essential question here is the power of the keys. Who possesses them? In the Gospels, it is a ministry, an instituted task, to go out and convert sinners. Christ does not wait for sinners to come to him. He goes out to them, the lost sheep.[80] And Christ incorporates others (e.g., the apostles) into this ministry. For instance, there is the institutional moment of Christ with his apostles on Easter Sunday: "Receive the Holy Spirit. If you forgive the sins of any, they are forgiven; if you retain the sins of any, they are retained."[81] And, as Saint Paul said,

> God ... through Christ reconciled us to himself and gave us the ministry of reconciliation; that is, in Christ God was reconciling the world to himself, not counting their trespasses against them, and entrusting to us the message of reconciliation. So we are ambassadors for Christ, God making his appeal through us. We beseech you on behalf of Christ, be reconciled to God.[82]

Christ's Gospel pattern for repentance is a top-down approach: God reconciles through Christ, who reconciles through his ministers, who reconcile sinners.

The sinner living the virtue of penance, the sinner trying to make amends will seek out Christ's structure for forgiveness. That structure works top-down. The sinner's living of the virtue of penance is a response to this ministry—indeed, to the Gospel—and it requires fitting into the hierarchical structure of that ministry.[83] So, God is working in both directions, from the top and bottom, bouncing the priest and penitent back and forth in their respective roles toward the penitent's forgiveness. A top-down approach, the preaching of repentance, leads to a bottom-up approach, the

---

79. Luke 19:8.

80. "The Son of man came to seek and to save the lost" (Luke 19:10). See also 1 Tim 1:15.

81. John 20:22–23.

82. 2 Cor 5:18–20.

83. See James 5:19–20: "If any one among you wanders from the truth and some one brings him back, let him know that whoever brings back a sinner from the error of his way will save his soul from death and will cover a multitude of sins."

virtue of penance, which must seek out and work with the top-down, the priest's absolution, in order to achieve its final goal, the forgiveness of sin.

We can see indirect indications in the New Testament of the ecclesial (or bottom-up) dimension of the individual living of repentance. One can think of the prodigal son, who cannot limit his conversion to his own cognizance of his fault but who must seek out his father.[84] The penitent woman who cleans Jesus's feet with her tears and hair did not stay comfortably at home.[85] The good thief on his cross manifests externally his repentance to the good Savior on the Cross.[86] The Letter of Saint James says, "Therefore confess your sins to one another, and pray for one another, that you may be healed."[87] The First Letter of Saint John says, "If we confess our sins, [God] is faithful and just, and will forgive our sins and cleanse us from all unrighteousness."[88]

However, I know of no explicit Scriptural proof mandating external confession to a priest. It is an implicit result from the top-down structure of salvation. The virtue of penance provides a moral explanation for the sacramental, liturgical requirement of a priest's absolution, or at least the intention to so seek out a priest. Using the Scholastic language of the virtues, we could say that it is an integral part of the virtue of penance to do whatever is necessary in order to sorrow and satisfy for one's sins.[89] Depending upon the era of salvation history, the form of external confession can vary, as Saint Thomas says: "the determination of the circumstances—when, how, and what one ought to confess, and to whom—this [part] in confession exists from the institution of divine law."[90] In all of this, one can properly say that external confession to a priest is an "act elicited" from the virtue of penance. This act of penance intends to enunciate past sins that are now rejected and for which forgiveness is implored.[91]

---

84. Luke 15:11–32.
85. Luke 7:37–50.
86. Luke 23:39–43.
87. Jas 5:16.
88. 1 John 1:9.
89. Doronzo, *De poenitentia*, 1:356–57.
90. "Determinatio circumstantiarum quando et quomodo et quid confiteri oporteat et cui, hoc est ex institutione juris divini in confessione" (Aquinas, *Scriptum super libros Sententiarum*, lib. IV, d. 17, q. 3, a. 2, qla. 2, ad. 1).
91. Aquinas, *Scriptum super libros Sententiarum*, lib. IV, d. 17, q. 3, a. 2, qla. 3, corpus; Doronzo, *De poenitentia*, 2:345–47.

Conclusion

The Catholic sacrament of penance is a delicate, balanced structure. Aquinas helped to illustrate that balance. It has not always been so. Shortly after Aquinas, Blessed Duns Scotus said that the penitent's role was nonessential. The emphasis was back on the priest. Sometimes, in certain sectors of Catholic life, I see the same error. A person may wish to continue in a particular behavior that Christ and his church have identified as sinful, but nonetheless, the person says to himself, "If I just go to the right priest who will give me absolution, then I can continue my behavior." That has not solved the problem, however. Without the virtue of penance, without sorrow and contrition according to Christ's moral truths, the priest's words are meaningless.

The history of the practice of the sacrament of penance illustrates tensions of the private and the public. The virtue of penance may seem to fall on the side of the private, the individual. As this essay has illustrated, however, the virtue of penance can help explain not just the externalization of repentance but the interpersonalization of repentance, the communal and indeed vertical and ecclesial dimension of repentance. Externalization is good, but repentance does not simply mean saying prayers aloud in the privacy of one's bedroom. Rather, repentance is interpersonal, in that the penitent must overcome sinful selfishness and extend out in virtue to God and the entire church.

In recent decades, there has been a revival of virtue theory by both Christian and secular thinkers. At the beginning of this essay, I mentioned that the notion of virtue could be seen as antithetical to Christianity according to certain Evangelical and Reformed believers. Virtue here is seen as emblematic of human works in a dialectic of gospel versus works. Nonetheless, there are recent Protestant theologians who are proposing a kind of virtue theory as consonant with the gospel. For instance, there are the Lutheran Gilbert Meilaender, the Episcopalian Jennifer Herdt, Stanley Hauerwas (longtime Methodist, now Anglican or Episcopalian), and the United Methodist Elizabeth Agnew Cochran. This Protestant appropriation of the overall notion of virtue could provide an interesting intersection with our sacramental study. Is it not true that the Luther of the "Brief Exhortation to Confession" in the *Large Catechism* is proposing virtuous activity? He certainly is. To be sure, between a non-Catholic Christian virtue theory and the Catholic sacrament of penance, there would be differences. Gilbert Meilaender, for instance, is honest about the difficulties of trying to square

Lutheranism with virtue theory's appeal to repeated action toward moral improvement.

> Meilaender argues that the implication of elevating justification within the Christian life is that grace, for Lutherans, is "in no sense a power that enables us to become 'more and more' what God wills we should be," as grace is within Catholicism. Rather, grace is something that we receive "again and again" as we return to our supreme acceptance of Christ's righteousness experienced in justification.[92]

This is a serious Catholic-Evangelical difficulty with respect to the notion of virtue in general. But if virtue theory is accepted by Evangelicals and not identified as an evil works construct, then perhaps the Catholic-Evangelical difficulty with respect to the virtue of penance may be lighter. For we both agree with Luther's first thesis that "the entire life of believers [is] to be one of repentance."

---

92. Cochran, "Faith, Love, and Stoic Assent," 213n69, quoting Gilbert C. Meilaender, *The Freedom of a Christian: Grace, Vocation, and the Meaning of Our Humanity* (Grand Rapids: Brazos, 2006), 43–44.

4

Is Reconciliation Still Relevant? Reflections on a Theological Theme in an Era of Diversity and Inclusivity

John P. Burgess

IN 1967 I WAS thirteen years old. 1967, the year before the assassinations of Martin Luther King, Jr., and Robert F. Kennedy. And in 1967, my denomination, the Presbyterian Church (USA), adopted a new confession of faith. To emphasize the confession's relevance to the historical moment, its authors named it, well, the Confession of 1967. In one fell swoop, the church judged the historic confession of Presbyterianism in the United States, the seventeenth-century Westminster Confession of Faith, inadequate; the Confession of 1967 would now be the public face of a socially aware and politically active church. Rather than offering a comprehensive system of faith, C67, as it came to be nicknamed, took a central theological theme, reconciliation, as a mandate for the church's present mission. The God who has reconciled himself to us in Jesus Christ calls the church to work for reconciliation in a world of racial discrimination, international conflict, economic inequality, and sexual confusion.[1]

But times quickly change, and what seemed relevant in 1967 almost immediately became dated. For one thing, C67 still uses "man" and "men"

---

1. For the history and theology of the confession, see "Introduction to the Confession of 1967," in *Book of Confessions: Study Edition* (Louisville: Geneva, 1999).

to refer to humanity and "he" and "himself" for God, whereas the Presbyterian Church soon embraced a thoroughgoing inclusive language regime. For another, C67 assumes a church that thinks of itself as an influential social force—after all, membership in the Presbyterian Church was at its peak in the 1960s, and the Presbyterian Church was so prominent socially that *Time Magazine* reported on C67. Now, fifty years later, the Presbyterian Church has endured splits, losses in membership, and massive reductions in its national staff, and while some Presbyterians remain nostalgic, their glory days are long gone.

But perhaps the biggest change since 1967 has been the church's retreat from the language of reconciliation. By 1982, a prominent Presbyterian theologian was warning against equating reconciliation "with sentimental love by an upper middle-class church, a smoothing over of real differences and tensions, an avoidance of confrontation, conflict and prophetic protest."[2] The church would now have to reinterpret reconciliation through the lens of justice. Other voices used stronger language; they told us that what American society first needed was a revolution; after that, we could talk—perhaps—about reconciliation.

Today, we still hear calls for social reconciliation, but its content and its realization seem much more elusive than in 1967. The most recent Presbyterian confessional statement, the 1991 "Brief Statement of Faith," does not even use the word "reconciliation"; instead, we are told, we must "hear the voices of peoples long silenced" and commit ourselves to "justice." The theological zodiac has moved into the sign that we might call "diversity and inclusivity." Is reconciliation still relevant?

A recent mailing from my daughter's college features a photo of one of her classmates, a young woman from Apple Valley, Minnesota. She projects intelligence, enthusiasm, and charm. In the accompanying text, she tells us, "I've never been part of a community so actively committed to inclusion, and the loyal support and encouragement I receive in every facet of life here has been hugely inspiring." She continues, "My peers push me in formal class discussions, and the conversations carry me into the dining hall; they diversify my perspective daily." In public life today, we constantly hear the call for inclusion or inclusivity, on the one hand, and diversity or difference, on the other.

---

2. Daniel Migliore, "Jesus Christ, the Reconciling Liberator: The Confession of 1967 and Theologies of Liberation," in "Reconciliation and Liberation—The Confession of 1967," *Journal of Presbyterian History* 61/1 (1983) 39.

What is it about inclusivity-diversity that has become so compelling? The ideas are not new; how to relate the one and the many has been a philosophical conundrum since the ancient Greeks. What is new is that these specific words now permeate our everyday language so thoroughly. Somehow, diversity and inclusivity no longer represent a perplexing metaphysical problem, but rather a practical solution to the deep human longing for community. Has inclusivity/diversity become a secular equivalent to what the church once called reconciliation? Or does it represent an alternative way of conceiving social solidarity?

At first, inclusivity and diversity seem to contradict each other.[3] Inclusivity suggests affirmation of others without regard to their background, ability, or identity. If I am included, I don't have to justify myself. I am valued just as I am. I possess an inherent dignity that others must respect. In contrast, diversity means that we are not just all alike. Diversity asks me not simply to accept others because they have the same worth as I, but rather to appreciate and value others because they have something that I don't: a different set of experiences or perspectives, a different social location or identity, from my own. The language of inclusivity invites us to become blind to the differences between us, whereas the language of diversity elevates the differences and asks us to become more aware of them.

But today we think of inclusivity and diversity as complementing each other. An organization that is inclusive of difference will be stronger, we are told, because difference enhances creativity. By listening to each other's unique experiences and perspectives, we come to more insight and better solutions than we would otherwise. According to the webpage of a major North American bank, "Diversity is the mix, and inclusion is the mix working well together." It goes on: "The business imperative is clear. . . . [Our] workforce and our client base are becoming more diverse each year, and in our view, to serve our markets, we must reflect our markets." So, "Organizations and societies can gain a competitive advantage by maximizing the potential of diverse workforces and teams."[4]

A recent article in *Forbes* magazine asserts that diversity and inclusion are the top business priority.[5] We read that "research now proves that

---

3. See Charles Taylor, *Multiculturalism and "The Politics of Recognition"* (Princeton: Princeton University Press, 1992).

4. Royal Bank of Canada, "RBC Diversity and Inclusion Blueprint 2020," https://www.rbc.com/diversity-inclusion/_assets-custom/includes/pdf/rbc-diversity-blueprint.pdf. See esp. 5.

5. Josh Bersin, "Why Diversity and Inclusion Will Be a Top Priority for 2016."

companies with great diversity outperform their peers by a significant margin." According to one study, "gender-diverse companies are 15% more likely to outperform their peers and ethnically-diverse companies are 35% more likely to do the same." Another study demonstrates that "inclusive teams outperform their peers by 80% in team-based assessments." No wonder then that the language of inclusivity and diversity appears so prominently in higher education. Even elite colleges and universities have become largely about preparing young people for managerial tasks in a globalized world.

What, though, can we observe about the fundamental assumptions behind this language? For one thing, note that this kind of diversity relates to a person's social identity, not to his or her ability to perform the work for which he or she is being hired. The language of inclusivity does not challenge the cruel meritocracy of our time. Second, it is assumed that a culture of inclusion necessarily results in greater cooperation and productivity, not that diversity and difference may result in interpersonal tension and even intractable disagreement. Third, if such tensions do arise, it is not the idea of diversity and inclusivity that needs critique; rather, particular individuals have failed to embrace others' differences, and these offenders must be corrected. We are very close here to what we call an ideology, which for all its talk about inclusivity can be ruthlessly judgmental and punitive.

So, the language of inclusivity and diversity is deeply managerial. It provides a practical way to negotiate relations among individuals who demand public recognition and affirmation of the distinctive identities that they have claimed for themselves. Perhaps diversity/inclusivity is also a typical American impulse. It is in our national DNA to celebrate pluralism, even as we assert *e pluribus unum*: the one and the many; unity and plurality; affirmation of the individual, as well as cooperation and community.

The language of inclusivity-diversity figured prominently when the Presbyterian Church last year added the Confession of Belhar to its confessional standards. The Confession of Belhar was composed in South Africa in the mid-1980s in theological protest against apartheid both within the South African churches and in South African society as a whole. Since then, it has been adopted by a number of European and North American churches.

Forbes, December 6, 2015. https://www.forbes.com/sites/joshbersin/2015/12/06/why-diversity-and-inclusion-will-be-a-top-priority-for-2016/#33e13a3b2ed5.

Repentance and Forgiveness

Like C67, the Confession of Belhar is oriented by the theological theme of reconciliation. But more strongly than C67, Belhar relates reconciliation to liberation and justice. And this combination—justice and reconciliation—has made Belhar attractive to many Presbyterians. They appeal to Belhar both to support the denomination's endorsement of same-sex marriage in 2015 (justice, inclusivity) and to call for those Presbyterians who have been alienated by that decision not to leave the denomination (reconciliation).

But if reconciliation matters, diversity and inclusivity matter even more. When the Presbyterian Church (USA) adopted the C67, it also created a Book of Confessions with nine historical documents from the early church, the Reformation, and the twentieth century. One powerful argument for Belhar was that the denomination would more fully represent its commitment to inclusivity and diversity by adopting a confession from outside of Europe or North America. The traditional Reformed theology of the Presbyterian Church (USA) would now be enriched by perspectives from the Third World.

The language of diversity/inclusivity deeply shapes our churches today. Whether in sermons from our pastors or in pronouncements from our denominational bodies, we hear more than ever these days about Jesus's meals with tax collectors and sinners; the breakthrough in the early church to table fellowship between Jewish and gentile Christians; and Paul's depiction of the church as a body whose different members nevertheless come together at the Lord's Supper. We now think of the church itself as the one and the many, as a unity based on a celebration of diversity.

The renewed focus on Christian table fellowship has, however, suggested a different, possibly richer image for social relationships: hospitality. Since 1967, the language of hospitality, like that of diversity/inclusivity, has become widely accepted, assumed, and authoritative in the Presbyterian Church (USA). Hospitality is a deeply biblical concept, and Christians have always practiced it, but now many American Christians regard hospitality as a strategy for managing social difference both within the church and in society as a whole.[6]

Today, people with diverse religious loyalties or no religious affiliation at all are in our congregations. A blended family may bring both baptized

---

6. The literature on Christian hospitality is immense. Key works include: Christine Pohl, *Making Room: Recovering Hospitality as a Christian Tradition* (Grand Rapids: Eerdmans, 1999), and Amos Yong, *Hospitality and the Other: Pentecost, Christian Practices, and the Neighbor* (Maryknoll: Orbis, 2008).

and unbaptized children; a Jewish man may accompany his Christian wife; or an unbaptized person may regularly attend a congregation without joining. When the Lord's Supper is celebrated, not only do these unbaptized persons frequently wish to participate, but many pastors and congregations also wish to include them, rather than to fence the table.

Just this year, the Presbyterian Church voted to remove baptism as a prerequisite for the Table. Now all people who put their trust in Jesus Christ are to be welcomed, although if an unbaptized person is regularly receiving the Supper, the pastor should invite him or her to receive baptism. One argument was simply practical: many congregations already practice an open table. But the fundamental argument was "hospitality," and it proved highly persuasive: the church is called by the Spirit to welcome the stranger, to overcome the social barriers that keep people apart, and to affirm that our differences do not divide but rather enrich us. Nowhere should that commitment to hospitality be more evident than at the Lord's Table.

Like diversity/inclusivity, the language of hospitality overlaps with C67's concern for reconciliation. But in contrast to diversity/inclusivity, hospitality more strongly emphasizes Christian virtues of humility and vulnerability. To make space for others, to invite them into table fellowship with me—that means also to be willing to learn from them, perhaps even to change my mind about the issues that divide us. If the language of diversity and inclusivity aims both at individual self-realization and at social cooperation, hospitality seeks what Christians call *koinonia*, a sense of mutual belonging and responsibility that neither eradicates personal identities nor overlooks genuine differences about fundamental theological or ethical issues.[7]

Unlike diversity/inclusivity, hospitality acknowledges that human separation and alienation are real. Like inclusivity-diversity, hospitality assumes that social solidarity is still possible if we are just friendly enough. But personal experience teaches that table fellowship does not by itself establish trusting, abiding friendship. Making space for another person does not necessarily mean that we will change our minds about the matters on which we disagree or that we will overcome the pain that we experience in each other's presence. The appeal to hospitality assumes that all that we need is personal goodwill to realize authentic community. But as important as our efforts are, they inevitably fall short. Offering—and accepting—hospitality

---

7. See Leanna K. Fuller, *When Christ's Body Is Broken* (Eugene, OR: Pickwick, 2016), 138–66.

never entirely escapes self-interest, either from the side of the host or the side of the guest.

Inclusivity and diversity. Hospitality. Each category has firmly established itself within the church and in society. If diversity and inclusivity have managerial connotations, hospitality, in contrast, touches the sphere of the interpersonal, the interrelational. Diversity/inclusivity aims at honoring people's different identities for the sake of mutual enrichment and corporate productivity, while hospitality seeks to cultivate trusting relationships that withstand interpersonal tension and disagreement. Both diversity/inclusivity and hospitality forms of social solidarity. But, again I ask: Are they also expressions of Christian reconciliation?

My assertion that diversity/inclusivity-diversity and hospitality have eclipsed reconciliation is, of course, exaggerated. Indeed, reconciliation has made a kind of comeback in recent years, especially in the political realm. In the wake of civil wars and the fall of totalitarian regimes, a number of countries have established so-called "truth and reconciliation commissions." A fascinating dimension of these commissions is their space for victims, for whom justice has finally been done, to look their victimizers fearlessly in the eye, while the victimizers express remorse and ask for forgiveness. Here we see a practical application of the insight that emerged after the adoption of the Confession of 1967: a traumatized society can bring about reconciliation among its members only after it has secured justice for the marginalized and oppressed.[8]

On the evening of November 9, 1989, the Berlin Wall fell. At that very moment, I was visiting my friends Harald and Beate Wagner on the outskirts of Leipzig, East Germany. In the 1970s, Harald spent nearly a year in prison for possessing books that had been smuggled in from the West. We are not talking about pornography, exposés of communist government corruption, or how to construct pipe bombs. Rather, this was the critical social analysis—and rather obtuse literature—of such philosophers as Herbert Marcuse, Theodor Adorno, and Jürgen Habermas. When the wall fell, people stormed the local offices of the Stasi, and someone found Harald's Stasi files and passed them on to him. Harald learned that a close friend—a man with whom he had shared and discussed these books—was his betrayer. Harald and Beate are deeply Christian people. They eventually confronted their friend as lovingly but truthfully as they could. At first, he denied everything; later, he refused to talk to them. Finally, he came back

---

8. See Miroslav Volf, *Exclusion and Embrace* (Nashville: Abingdon, 1996).

to them, deeply ashamed and almost broken psychologically. Harald and Beate offered forgiveness, but reconciliation did not really take place. The wounds on both sides were still too raw. Confession and forgiveness are apparently necessary but not sufficient for reconciliation to take place.

Truth and reconciliation commissions, like diversity/inclusivity and hospitality strategies, focus on what humans can and indeed must do to achieve social solidarity. But, as we have seen, each approach has limitations. Whether working from diversity/inclusivity, hospitality, or truth and reconciliation, humans quickly find that alongside genuine breakthroughs to cooperation and fellowship is the reality of intractable tensions, differences, and injustices: Israel and Palestine, Ferguson, Russia and Ukraine, the Presbyterian Church (USA) and the Presbyterian Church in America, and a politically polarized United States, just to begin a list. Christians commit themselves to reconciliation, but its realization on earth remains fragmentary and imperfect.[9]

Here the Confession of 1967 proves its continuing relevance. C67 makes clear that reconciliation is above all a theological category, not a managerial or interpersonal matter. Reconciliation involves something more than human aspirations for social solidarity; rather, reconciliation is first of all God's free and gracious act in Jesus Christ. Karl Barth speaks of the three tenses of salvation. Our reconciliation with God took place two thousand years ago at Golgotha; we receive it again whenever Word and sacrament penetrate our hearts; and we pray "Maranatha," asking that our Lord bring his reconciling work to consummation.

Diversity/inclusivity removes barriers to people's full participation in society by honoring their distinctive identities. Hospitality invites "the other" into my space in order to build trusting relationship. In contrast, reconciliation depends on confession and forgiveness of sin. But whereas truth and reconciliation strategies begin with the confession of violation that victimizers owe victims, a Christian understanding of reconciliation asks people first of all to make confession before God.

As he shaped a seminary of the German Confessing Church from 1935–37, Dietrich Bonhoeffer anticipated the dangers that threaten Christian community—the rivalries that inevitably emerge, the tendency for leaders to dominate and manipulate, and the temptation for a group to find its unity in a particular political ideology (or, in my city of Pittsburgh, the

---

9. See Kenneth Cragg, *This Year in Jerusalem* (London: Darton, Longman, and Todd, 1982), 142–43.

local sports teams, the Steelers or the Penguins!).[10] To keep his seminarians grounded in Christ and Christ's reconciling work, Bonhoeffer asked them to commit themselves to morning and evening prayer, mutual care and service, and celebration of the Lord's Supper. But what happens when tensions and disagreements nevertheless arise? What does a Christian community do when, despite its best, most disciplined efforts, it falls short of realizing Christian reconciliation—or as the apostle Paul says, when we fail to discern the body (1 Cor 11:29)?

Bonhoeffer did not deny the importance of holding each other accountable when we hurt each other and undermine social solidarity. Justice and truth are essential components of Christian community. But, for Bonhoeffer, our failures at reconciliation do not mean that we simply double down and try harder. Rather, we need nothing less than a miracle—the miracle that God so loved the world that he gave his only begotten Son that the world should not perish but have eternal life in him. "In him," in Christ, as the Apostle Paul declares (2 Cor 5:16), we no longer look at each other from a human point of view. "In him," in Christ, our unity does not depend on our success at either diversity/inclusivity or hospitality. "In Christ" means that the only thing—the *only* thing—that we have in common is the cross.[11] There, beneath the cross, I discover the most basic truth: that the other is a sinner, as am I; and that the other is one for whom Christ has died, as he has for me.

For Bonhoeffer, therefore, it is the reconciliation that God has accomplished in Jesus Christ that calls forth our confession—and not only our confession of sin—our helplessness, our weakness—but also our confession of faith: the joyous declaration that God remains true to his promises despite the brokenness that humans inflict on each other, the alienation that we experience in each other's presence, and the differences that we ourselves are unable to overcome. Bonhoeffer asked his seminarians to confess their sins to one another prior to their monthly reception of communion. The young men were resistant. Personal confession of sin from one Christian to another seemed too "Catholic," too "monastic." Finally, one evening prior

---

10. For what follows, see Dietrich Bonhoeffer, *Life Together/Prayerbook of the Bible*, ed. Geffrey B. Kelly, trans. Daniel B. Loesch and James H. Burtness (Minneapolis: Fortress, 1996).

11. See Markus Barth, *Ephesians* (Garden City: Doubleday, 1974), 281, 307–11.

to a communion Sunday, Bonhoeffer took one of the seminarians aside and asked him to hear Bonhoeffer's confession.[12]

No seminary professor today would dare do such a thing. I would be accused, perhaps rightfully so, of "violating boundaries," as they say. My dean would not defend me on the basis of diversity and inclusivity. No student would thank me for having offered him or her gracious hospitality. Indeed, seminaries constantly misuse such words as grace and hospitality to mean that I should accept late papers or give an "A" for "B" work. But Bonhoeffer's invitation for a student to hear his confession was, in fact, an act of inclusivity that exceeds what any progressive college or business practices today. It was an act of hospitality that far surpasses the table fellowship in the seminary cafeteria that I enjoy with students and colleagues, some of whom I like and others I don't. To expose my sinfulness to a Christian brother or sister—to reveal that I am not everything that I pretend to be or that others think that I am—is deeply painful yet, Bonhoeffer believed, immensely liberating.[13]

Note here that Bonhoeffer does not insist that I confess my sins directly to people whom I have violated. This is no truth and reconciliation commission. Rather, I am confessing my sins to God in the presence of a Christian brother or sister. And his or her task is neither to judge me not to offer pastoral counsel but simply to declare: "In Jesus Christ, you are forgiven." Reconciliation in this past tense makes possible its present tense, as together we come repentant and forgiven to the bread and the wine that we call Eucharist. This, says Bonhoeffer, is the highpoint of the community's life together.

But there is still the future tense of reconciliation, and that is why at the Table we pray, "Thy kingdom come."[14] Inclusivity and diversity do not require prayer; they involve management techniques. People who practice hospitality may pray but also maybe not; they don't want to offend their guests. Truth and reconciliation commissions do amazing work, but they do not ask victimizers and victims to pray together. But those who live by God's reconciling act in Jesus Christ fervently plead, "Thy kingdom come." In the past, God accepted us without regard to our merits; in the present,

---

12. Bonhoeffer, *Life Together*, 16.

13. In asking the church to examine its own failures in working for reconciliation, the Confession on 1967 moves along similar lines.

14. For the significance of this petition, see Karl Barth, *The Christian Life*, trans. Geoffrey W. Bromiley (Edinburgh: T. & T. Clark, 1981), 233–71.

Repentance and Forgiveness

God sets the table at which hosts and guests are truly brothers and sisters; and in the future, God will heal the wounds of Harald and Beate and their betrayer.

When we pray, "Thy kingdom come," we momentarily look away from our broken past and hurting present into God's perfected future: a heavenly banquet. "Thy kingdom come" makes reconciliation relevant in an era of diversity and inclusivity—because only a church that prays for the kingdom to enter into the very heart of its existence can truly be socially aware and politically active, and otherwise it will be useless.

The Confession of 1967 declares, "With an urgency born of this hope the church applies itself to present tasks and strives for a better world. It does not identify limited progress with the kingdom of God on earth, nor does it despair in the face of disappointment and defeat. In steadfast hope the church looks beyond all partial achievement to the final triumph of God." Reconciliation is ultimately in God's hands, not ours. It is, as theologians like to say, an eschatological reality. And, yet, this future impinges on the present. It impels us to seek reconciliation with each other, a reconciliation that is more than diversity/inclusivity and more than hospitality—because it is the solidarity of those who cry out together for God to make right what they cannot.

With that, C67 comes to a close—well, almost. For there is still one thing that it has to confess; indeed, all that any Christian can finally say, although, of course, the most important thing. May I offer the words of Ephesians, the great letter of reconciliation, also to you? "Now to him who by the power at work within us is able to do far more abundantly than all we ask or think, to him be the glory in the church and in Jesus Christ to all generations forever and ever. Amen."

5

"I Am the Foremost of Sinners" (1 Tim 1:15): Negotiating the Church's Language of Self-Condemnation[1]

Peter C. Bouteneff

ONE OF THE PRECONDITIONS of repentance is the acknowledgement of one's own sin. There is no turning, no change of heart, no *metanoia*, without the realization that we are broken. So repentance—itself a precondition for our entry and constant reentry into genuine human life—is itself predicated on our seeing ourselves as fallen. As sinful. As persons in need of healing and forgiveness. Otherwise, what is there to repent of?

Immediately after Pentecost, Peter addresses the Judeans. Filled with the Holy Spirit, he preaches to them, citing the scriptures to show who Jesus is—Lord and Christ. And before Peter tells them to repent and be baptized, the book of Acts reports about his listeners that they were "cut to the heart" (Acts 2:37). And they ask what to do, and then Peter tells them to repent and be baptized.

Likewise, though perhaps less obviously, forgiveness too depends on the realization of our own sin. The Lord's Prayer connects God's forgiveness of our shortcomings with our forgiveness of others'. "Forgive us our trespasses as we forgive those who trespass against us"—this is either telling

---

1. This talk draws on material from my book *How to Be a Sinner: Finding Yourself in the Ancient Language of Repentance* (Yonkers: St. Vladimir's Seminary Press, 2018).

Repentance and Forgiveness

God to *imitate our forgiveness* ("Our Father: do as we do!"), which is somewhat preposterous, or it is our pledge to be in the business of forgiving others, as a condition of our asking forgiveness of God. All of which to say that if we are not aware of our own sin and indebtedness before God and others, we are neither in a position to ask forgiveness, nor are our hearts kindled to forgive others.

So a crucial part of the dynamic of Christian life—at our entry into it and in our constant re-commitment to it—is to be cut to the heart, to realize the need for repentance and forgiveness, aligning ourselves with God's reconciliation (2 Cor 2:18–20).

God, the supremely merciful one, removes our sins from us, as far as the East is from the West, for his love is as great the height of the heavens above the earth (Ps 103:11–12); he reconciles and forgives, regardless of our state of repentance. Yet repentance is also required of us. Jesus consistently praises the posture of compunction—it is the repentant publican who returns home justified, and not the haughty Pharisee (Luke 18:14). The father of the prodigal, we might imagine, has forgiven his son from the moment his son even asks for his inheritance. Yet the real feast begins when the son, having repented, returns of his own accord back to the father's loving embrace.

When it comes to our reconciling with each other, as friends, as spouses, as colleagues, we know the ontological change that occurs when the person we are trying to forgive comes to us and acknowledges their fault. Or if we are the offending party, then our own acknowledgment of wrong transforms and liberates *us* as well. When Jesus says to his disciples, "If you forgive the sins of any, they are forgiven; if you retain the sins of any, they are retained" (John 20:23), we are mindful that this can be taken as a specific word to the inner circle, in view of their future ministries. But we can also take these words universally. When we "retain" sins of our own or of other people, everyone is held back by this retention. When we forgive, everyone is freed. Our forgiveness and God's are indeed bound up with each other—to return again to the logic of the Lord's prayer.

My first premise, therefore, is simply that an acknowledgment of our own sins is a vital part of genuine human life. Both as a precondition of repentance and forgiveness, but even before that, because our self-understanding as sinners constitutes a truthful appraisal of our state of being. In other words, the reason to consider ourselves sinners, unworthy of divine love and reconciliation, is primarily that it is *true*. And our living in truth will be a living in wholeness, and as we'll be seeing, a living in peace, joy, and compassion, living in the constant awareness of our being forgiven, undeservingly, by the loving God.

Continuing in a spirit of personal reflection (rather than academic analysis), I would like to examine further what it means to reckon ourselves as sinners, to explore the uses and abuses of what we may rightly call the *sinner identity*. For the scriptures and the prayer life of most of our churches is full of language that has us adopting and owning the name of "sinner." And my premise is that exploring the potential problems of employing the sinner language about ourselves, adopting the posture of self-condemnation (while also examining the ways that these can go wrong), will help us enter more fully into its immense spiritual gifts.

The Sinner Identity and Its Problems

Everyone sins. "None is righteous, no, not one" (Rom 3:10). That must include me. "If we say we are sinless we deceive ourselves" (1 John 1:8). In other words, I am deluded if I do not recognize the fact that I sin, and that I am *a sinner*. The aforementioned publican identifies himself that way, and is praised by Jesus. Paul says still more about himself: "I am the *foremost* of sinners" (1 Tim 1:15).

Following these realities into the early church's prayer tradition, the sinner language and the sinner identity continue most clearly and consistently in the prayer we know as "The Jesus Prayer." In the fullest of its several forms, this prayer reads, "Lord, Jesus Christ, Son of God, have mercy upon me a sinner." This petition accompanies a huge number of Christians to this day, who repeat, hundreds or even thousands of times in a given day, "Lord, Jesus Christ, Son of God, have mercy on me, a sinner."

The Orthodox Church's liturgical and prayer tradition features entire canons (sets of prayers and refrains, lasting pages) devoted to the identification of our sinfulness and the asking of God's mercy. One of them, the Great Canon of Saint Andrew of Crete (recited in many of our churches in its entirety at the beginning of Lent), begins by asking, "How shall I begin to mourn the deeds of my wretched life?" And it continues by naming every biblical sinner from Adam onwards, seeing my own sins as worse than theirs:

Repentance and Forgiveness

> David . . . first murdered a man and then stole his wife—
> but was quick to repent of both.
> You, however, my soul, have done worse things than he,
> yet never repented of them before the Lord.
>
> I am the worst sinner in the world.[2]

Most of our denominations feature, in their private and public prayer life, confession of sins, often with the acknowledgment that we are sinners. Sometimes with qualifiers such as "wretched."

Before saying more about the immense *value* of owning up to our sin, and even adopting the identity of "sinner," I would like to problematize this idea. Because not only are there several neurotic ways to conceive of ourselves as wretched sinners, there are also logical, theological, and pastoral problems with that self-condemnation whose identification and discussion may be profitable, on the way to discovering how naming myself a sinner, and owning that identity in the face of a loving, merciful God, can be a critical, indispensable part of our healing. The proper self-regard, *as sinner*, is the key to repentance, forgiveness, and reconciliation, but also to a powerful humility, to inner peace, to compassion for others, and to the impossibility of judging anyone.

Here is an outline of the problems I seek to name and discuss here:

1. Can the "sinner language" be either neurotic or even deeply harmful? Can naming myself a "sinner," thus giving me that fixed identity, potentially enshrine my sinful behavior? What if, through much of my life, and especially in my childhood, I was told that I am worthless, that I don't amount to anything, that I'm garbage? Can calling myself a "wretched sinner" awaken or perpetuate self-destructive messages?

2. What is this "sinful self?" Is it the totality of myself? Or is there a part of myself that's bad? Or do I have two selves, a good and bad one?

3. Finally, what about a proper self-love and self-care? Am I not supposed to love myself, as a creature of God, made in his image? Is not "low self-esteem" at the root of many personal and societal problems?

---

2. See in Kallistos Ware and Mother Mary, trans., *The Lenten Triodion* (London: Faber, 1978).

Problems of the Sinner Identity: The Power of the Name

We need not go very deeply into semiotic theory to understand that the act of naming things has great significance. Calling myself something, giving myself a name, like "sinner," has significance. The act of naming has important implications that are testified within Scripture. Adam's being given charge to name all the animals had deep significance for the human person's relationship to the natural world (Gen 2:19). God himself is seen to change the names of certain people at the turning points of their lives: Abram becomes Abraham, Simon becomes Peter, Saul becomes Paul. The name is both a sign and also a carrier of power. The name of Jesus is "the name by which we are saved."[3] And each of the many names by which Jesus is known has a precise meaning.[4]

Names both identify us and also affect who we are. So we ought to reflect on the power of calling ourselves "sinner." For example, let's imagine that during the formative years of my life, people regularly called me "a miserable mistake," or my parents hit me, abused me, or I have been sexually assaulted. Then isn't calling myself "a sinner" and "a wretch" going to be deeply harmful, when what I really need is healing and building up? Indeed it could. And thoughtful spiritual guidance may be necessary in such cases, where someone may well be advised against the use of "sinner" language for a considerable period. Or where such language is deployed in a mindful way, under the counsel of someone experienced with the phenomenon of abuse.

But even for those who do not carry such painful associations, the wider question remains: If I call myself a "sinner," am I giving that word a power over myself? Am I in danger of letting the word "sinner" become *part of my truest identity*? Does the name and identity of "sinner" *entrap* me into sinful behavior, by enshrining it in a title?

I think that these are appropriate questions, and they lead us to reflect on the different kinds of effects names have on us. Because names and categories do not necessarily determine us. Meyers-Briggs categories, for example, ideally do not have a deterministic effect on our lives; rather they help identify some tendencies in how we act and react. We are always free

---

3. Acts 2:21; 4:12.

4. See Thomas Hopko, *The Names of Jesus: Discovering the Person of Christ through Scripture* (Chesterton, IN: Ancient Faith, 2015).

Repentance and Forgiveness

to perceive and act and live *outside* these markers, transcend them. But their transcendence relies on their first being identified.

Could we not say the same for being a sinner? The transcendence of sin (through repentance) must begin with its identification. Name it. Claim it. Confess it. Repent of it. Surrender it to God, in community with other sinners.

Another significant and relevant place where we can gain insight on this question of "naming" is within the world of addiction. One of the first steps in the treatment of addictions, especially within the Twelve-Step world, involves *identifying yourself* as an addict. As you begin your recovery, and at every single meeting, you identify yourself, saying, "I am an alcoholic." "I am a sex-addict." "I am a drug addict." Here too, one may wonder, are such people surrendering to these identities? Letting these identities shape their behavior?

The amazing thing here is, *yes,* an alcoholic *is* surrendering to her identity as alcoholic. But if she's doing it right, it's not in a way that will lead her to drink. First of all, "I am an alcoholic," or in our case, "I am a sinner," simply means "I have a problem." "I am unwell." I am not saying that "alcoholic/sinner defines the totality of who I am." I am saying that *I am not whole.* And this is hugely significant. This self-perception, and this self-identification, identifies an alcoholic who is being healed, rather than one who isn't—and there is a vast gulf between the two.

Furthermore, as one Christian author puts it, "The statement 'I am an alcoholic' means, 'I am not God,' or even, 'I am not God, [and therefore] *someone else must be.*"[5] And since someone else is God, the addict is free to let God work in his life, and to cooperate with that work.

By linking the addict-identity with the sinner-identity, I do not mean in any way to imply that being an addict is itself sinful. It is not. But the understanding and confession of my identity—"I am an addict" or "I am a sinner"—is the understanding and confession that I have a problem, and I alone cannot get myself out of it. I am not fully in control. I must submit to God, who *is* in control. Understood this way, saying "I am a sinner" means, "God, your will be done."

The ideas above draw on a perceptive book about the twelve steps by an Orthodox priest. The same author points out that the name and title of "alcoholic" is worn as a badge of honor, giving the bearer a sense of

---

5. Meletios Webber, *Steps of Transformation: An Orthodox Priest Explores the Twelve Steps* (Ben Lomond, CA: Conciliar Press), 58.

belonging in a group where everyone bears that title."[6] Translating that into the language of "sinner," we can say that calling myself "sinner" is part of my acknowledgment of the problem, my submission to God, and also my badge of identification as a member of the Church, the hospital for sinners. Because *all who are in the church are sinners*. And our way forward in Christ, our way towards freedom from sin, is something that we work out both by ourselves, and in community with each other.

So, far from entrapping me, the self-descriptive of "sinner" should be seen as a realistic and healing *surrender*, a *liberation*. It is an admission of my brokenness, my yielding of power to God. It is also a sign of my membership in a community that is both already the body of Christ, and also constantly becoming that body, through the healing of sin, the mending of brokenness, the restoration of the divine image. It is a community of broken persons who know that their wholeness rests entirely in Christ and is dependent entirely upon God.

Why does Christ say that the tax collectors and harlots will enter the kingdom before the temple priests who were interrogating him (Matt 21:31)? Because they *know* they are sinners; at least the ones in Jesus's company did. The "moral" ones, who believe they are following all the rules correctly, are the most difficult to save (and also the most insufferable people). Jesus's parables and preaching—and his choice of the company he keeps—are consistent on that message.

Problems of the Sinner Identity: What Is My Sinful Self?

Having established the potential benefits of naming ourselves "sinner," we would take some of those same questions further: Does "sinner" define the totality of who I am? Is my self an innately sinning entity?

This question is made all the more stark by the conviction that I, myself, my self, am made in the image of God. When I consider my true self, therefore, is it not truly good and beautiful, worthy of loving care more than condemnation?

Or do I somehow have *two selves*, a sinful self to be denied and hated, and an image-bearing self that is to be encouraged and loved? In which case, how many people am I? Or are there *parts* of myself to love, cherish, and be true to, and parts to be ignored, denied, hated . . . even died to?

---

6. Meletios Webber, *Steps of Transformation: An Orthodox Priest Explores the Twelve Steps* (Ben Lomond, CA: Conciliar Press), 58.

Repentance and Forgiveness

The self is not a monolith; it is a complex thing. Saint Paul reflects on this conundrum—the conflicting "parts" of himself—in his stirring confession in the Epistle to the Romans. Recall Paul's exasperation in Romans 7:15—8:2, emphasis added.: "I do not understand my own actions. For I do not do what I want, but I do the very thing I hate. . . . *But in fact it is no longer I that do it, but sin that dwells within me.*"

This is an inner conflict that we can all relate to: I know what is right, but I don't do it. It is as if there is something foreign living in me, called "sin."

"I can *will* what is right, but I cannot *do* it. For I do not do the good I want, but the evil I do not want is what I do. Now if I do what I do not want, it is no longer I that do it, but sin that dwells within me."

Again, "sin" dwells within me, like a force, a virus.

"So I find it to be a law that when I want to do what is good, evil lies close at hand. *For I delight in the* law *of God, in my inmost self* [κατὰ τὸν ἔσω ἄνθρωπον], but I see in my members another law at war with the law of my mind and making me captive to the law of sin that dwells in my members."

Crucially, even as he says he doesn't do what he knows is right, he also says that he has an *inmost self* that delights in the law of God.

So all is not lost. Our inmost or true self also delights in God and his law. Our inmost self is good and true. We are not totally depraved. But we are deeply confused. And sin exists in order to confuse us.

Finally, we see that although Paul is exasperated, he also knows he is *saved*: "Wretched man that I am! Who will rescue me from this body of death? Thanks be to God through Jesus Christ our Lord! . . . There is therefore now no condemnation for those who are in Christ Jesus. For the law of the Spirit of life in Christ Jesus *has set you free* from the law of sin and of death."

Christ has set us free. It is done; it is consummated. But as important as it is to know and trust our God-given freedom, we also must recall that we are still confused. We are torn, as if in two. Both of these realities—salvation and confusion, brokenness and healing, forgiveness and sin—have to be kept before us.

But let us return to what Paul calls our inmost self, our most true self: it is indeed *good*, and delights in God, in whose image it is made.

Nikolai of Zhicha, a twentieth-century Serbian saint, also speaks of the inner person, the inner self, that also tells us something about the right kind of self-love:

> When a person loves only himself, he loves neither God nor his fellow-people. He does not even love the person that is in himself; he loves only his thoughts about himself, his illusions about himself. Were he to love the person in himself, he would love God's image in him, and would quickly become a lover of God and man, for he would be seeking man and God in other people, as objects of his love.

Together with what Paul says in Romans, the above reflection confirms that in fact I am not two "selves"; I am one self, one whole person, one "I." This person, who is made in the image and glory of God, is the self-same person who gives in to evil, sullying the universe with his impure thoughts and shameful deeds. I am a single, beautiful-but-broken self, and my freedom in Christ begins by acknowledging this very thing.

Self-Esteem and Self-Love

Another question we may raise about the "sinner identity" is, if I am a wretched sinner, how can I love myself? What about healthy self-esteem, and self-care?

This question is raised especially if we read the ascetical literature, such as the Philokalia, that regularly tells us—in the English translation—to "flee self-esteem." The warning arises frequently: avoid self-esteem as if you are fleeing demons.

Whenever we read biblical or ancient texts, or anything that has been translated from another language, we do well to be attentive to the words, and—to the extent we can know it—what they actually meant in their language and context. So when we look at the Greek word that is usually translated as "self-esteem," what do we find? What are we supposed to flee? *Kenodoxia*. *Keno* meaning "empty" as in "kenosis," and *doxia* meaning "glorification." A much better—indeed, literal—translation would be vainglory.

So we are not necessarily supposed to flee any and all self-esteem. We are to flee vainglory, our *attachment* to self-esteem, our addiction to caring what others think and say about us, our image in the world. The ascetical texts are telling us, "*Flee that imprisonment* to yourself. Flee, also, your imprisonment to your own will, to getting what you want. That is a prison. Submit, rather, in love, submit to God, and to the other."

What then about self-love? Here we would recall what was said above about our self and our "innermost person." When we have that right sense of who we are, we come to understand that our genuine self, created in God's holy image, is to be cherished, nurtured, respected, and loved.

I believe the self-love that the penitential texts tell us to avoid, to flee, is rather *self-obsession*. And the ancient ascetical writers knew that danger, but could scarcely have imagined how our contemporary society would drive us so powerfully towards self-obsession.

The Sweetness of Compunction

With the above, we have (briefly) problematized the sinner identity and, where possible, de-problematized it. We have also examined some of the ancient texts for what they are saying about self-esteem and self-love. I would like now to close with some positive statements, where the ancients tell us about what we actually have to *gain* by considering ourselves sinners.

Here I would focus on two reasons that the sinner identity is healthy, and both of these come into focus only when we consider, well, *God*.

First, the sinner identity, as I said in the beginning, is healthy because it is the truth. To the extent we consider ourselves before the face of great and ever-loving God, this truth becomes increasingly apparent. Indeed, when we look at ourselves, not only before the face of God, but before the face of anything that is truly good, pure, honest, and beautiful (Phil 4:8), we are apt to realize our brokenness, fallenness, and sinfulness. Recognizing this truth is a deeply healthy thing, a therapeutic thing.

Second, the sinner identity is healthy when we consider that God is *merciful*. He *is* mercy. This is what makes our self-condemnation not only tolerable, survivable, but beautiful. Especially when we consider that God works specifically in and through brokenness. To paraphrase both Rumi and Leonard Cohen, "The cracks are where the light gets in." Paul writes, I am the foremost of sinners; *but I received mercy for this reason* (1 Tim 1:15–16). This is the dynamic embedded in our broken-redeemed world. As Gregory of Nazianzus would put it, "God heals in no more certain way than through suffering and humiliation [κακοπάθεια]," and then he continues, "God's love for us is the counterpart of [our] tears."[7]

The positive dimensions of the sinner identity are revealed especially in the light of God's limitless love, his mercy, his forgiveness. So that when I consider my sin, with an even *partial* knowledge of God's endless love,

---

7. Gregory of Nazianzus, *Or. Bas.* 24.11.

God's boundless mercy, God's total forgiveness, I experience a shower of benefits:

> I open the doors of repentance—and therefore to forgiveness and reconciliation.
> I cease being in denial of my brokenness.
> I become an increasingly whole person.
> I become merciful to other people. And to myself.
> I find it impossible and absurd to judge or condemn someone else.
> I find it impossible and absurd to take offense at things people say and do.
> I lose my obsession with what others think of me.
> I am at liberty.
> I find creativity.
> Because I understand that it is no longer I who live, but Christ lives in me.
> Christ loves in me.

In all this, we find the joy of repentance, even the joy of compunction. Listen to some insights from Saint John Climacus: "The one who wears blessed, God-given mourning like a wedding garment gets to know the spiritual laughter of the soul."[8]

As I ponder the true nature of compunction, I find myself amazed by the way in which inward joy and gladness mingle with mourning and grief, like honey in a comb. There must be a lesson here, and it surely is that *compunction is properly a gift from God*, so that there is a real pleasure in the soul, since God secretly brings consolation to those who in their heart of hearts are repentant.[9]

The repentant are full of consolation and joy, because they know who they are and they know the mercy of God. All of this helps to explain why—quite consistently in the ancient prayer texts—we actually *ask* God for tears of compunction.

Owning the sinner identity—the identity of *the forgiven sinner*—can be fraught with problems, with potential neuroses. But when it is done right, with an increasing knowledge of both self and God, it is the key to our salvation and our joy.

---

8. Colm Luibheid and Norman Russell, trans., *John Climacus: The Ladder of Divine Ascent*, Classics of Western Spirituality (New York: Paulist, 1982), 140.

9. Luibheid and Russell, *John Climacus*, 141.

6

Confession and Repentance in the Emerging Technoculture

Brent Waters

SIN HAS BEEN A perennial constant in the human condition, so is there anything all that novel or interesting about confessing and repenting in our current circumstances? Sin is sin, always has been and always will be. I believe, however, that the emerging technoculture in which you and I live does present some unique challenges, because context goes a long way in shaping what we confess and how we repent. Before exploring these challenges, however, I need to do two things: 1) explain, briefly, what I mean by confession, repentance, and forgiveness; and 2) describe the context of the emerging technoculture.

To confess is to acknowledge a wrong committed against God or neighbor without appealing to any excuse. Following C. S. Lewis,[1] we often confuse confessing with looking for an alibi. Our so-called prayers of confession are really descriptions of extenuating circumstances that caused us to make a mistake. But the point of confession is to admit committing a wrong that should not be excused. If you have an excuse, then there is nothing to forgive. Confession necessarily entails divulging the inexcusable.

---

1. C. S. Lewis, *The Weight of Glory: And Other Addresses* (N.p.: HarperCollins, 2009), 179–82. Ebook.

Repentance is the desire to right the wrong committed. We are sorry, for instance, that we have harmed a neighbor, and we wish to mend that which we have broken. To repent is to take responsibility for the inexcusable act we have committed. It is the contrite expression of heartfelt remorse.

Forgiveness, in part, is accepting a contrite apology, but it also entails much more. Forgiving and promising cannot, or should not, be separated. Following Hannah Arendt,[2] one is not entitled to be forgiven for the act one has confessed and repented. Since only that which should be punished can be forgiven, there must also be a promise to change one's behavior so the punishable act is not repeated. Arendt admits that a great deal of ambiguity accompanies such promising and forgiving, because we cannot know whether promises will be kept in the future. But she prefers the uncertainty of promising and forgiving over the certainty of revenge as an alternative for righting wrongs. Moreover, she captures the gist of the Eucharistic liturgy in which absolution is not pronounced until there is the promise of amending one's life.

Confession, repentance, and forgiveness are not of much use if they are simply abstract ideas. They take on their meaning within specific settings, and these vary over time and locale. How forgiveness, for instance, is understood and practiced in an ancient Christian household differs from its contemporary counterparts within differing cultures and social settings. So what does it mean to confess, repent, and forgive in the emerging technoculture? Before I can answer this question, I must spend some time describing this context.

You and I live in an emerging technoculture. By this I do not mean the growing collection of gadgets and devices that clutter our lives. Rather, the ubiquitous presence of technology shaping the fabric of daily life reveals an underlying drive of mastery. George Grant proclaims: "In each lived moment of our waking and sleeping, we are technological civilisation."[3] These waking and sleeping moments disclose an obsessive drive for asserting greater mastery over nature and human nature. Grant's references to "nature" and "human nature" are cryptic, but what he has in mind is the late modern project of creating a world more amenable to human purposes.

---

2. See Hannah Arendt, *The Human Condition* (Chicago: University of Chicago Press, 1998), 236–43, and Hannah Arendt, *The Promise of Politics* (New York: Shocken, 2005), 52–62.

3. George Parkin Grant, *Technology and Justice* (Notre Dame: Notre Dame University Press, 1986), 11.

Repentance and Forgiveness

In the "will to mastery," humans make things happen.[4] Through employing technology, humans transform nature into resources that both expand the range of available options, while diminishing the threat of chance or randomness. Asserting such mastery is thereby relentless and progressive, as reflected in the late modern belief that the chief accomplishments of a civilization are measured by its ability to construct and control the future. The world into which we are born is not a given, but a human artifact. Again, as Arendt recognized, the world "is the result of human productivity and human action."[5] The world "is not identical with the earth or with nature," but a "human artifact, the fabrication of human hands."[6] In short, it is through technology that humans create a world as their suitable habitat for being human.

Asserting such mastery, however, is not an extrinsic act, but unleashes the will to mastery as intrinsic to being human. It is in this willing that humans free themselves from the constraints of nature and human nature to become more fully human.[7] Consequently, nature and human nature are effectively transformed into artifacts of the will. Nature is little more than raw material that may be used or abused, cherished or despised in accordance to its assigned valuation. Pristine wilderness may be farmed, mined, developed, or preserved, but each instance is the outcome of what is willed. Human nature as well is an artifact of the will. Behavior, for instance, is controlled through incentives and disincentives, therapy, drugs, and perhaps someday extensive genetic modification.

Even such universal natural events as birth and death are increasingly subjected to technological control. Fetal development is routinely monitored, and in some instances tested. Infertility can be overcome through drugs, gamete donation, artificial insemination, in-vitro fertilization (IVF), and surrogacy. A variety of techniques—such as fetal screening and abortion, or IVF and preimplantation genetic diagnosis (PGD)—may be used to prevent the birth of children with severe illnesses or disabilities. More broadly, these same technologies may be employed to avoid undesirable traits or select desirable ones. Should safe and reliable technologies be developed, selected genetic traits may someday be enhanced. At the end

---

4. Grant, *Technology and Justice*, 12–13.
5. Arendt, *Promise of Politics*, 107.
6. Arendt, *Human Condition*, 52.
7. See Hannah Arendt, *The Life of the Mind, Volume Two: Willing* (San Diego: Harcourt, 1978), 3–5.

of life, various drugs and medical procedures alleviate pain. Increasingly, death itself is becoming more a matter of choice than necessity. Patients can choose to prolong their lives, delay their deaths, or be assisted in dying at a time and means of their choosing. The beginning and end of life, as well as the time in between, are now more artifacts of the will than a natural unfolding of a human life.

The will is the central feature of the identities of those inhabiting the emerging technoculture, and for the will to fully assert itself, it should be as free as possible from any external or unwanted constraints. Consequently, mobility, both physical and imaginative, is a premium value. Those populating the emerging culture—you and I and the people we know and love—are a nomadic people. By "nomadic" I am referring to those who, with the assistance of information and transportation technologies, do not perceive physical location as a determinative or decisive factor in respect to their work, leisure, or identity. For these late modern nomads, any distinction between "local" and "remote" has become blurred. In short, the nomads inhabiting the emerging technoculture perceive the world as a place they may wander as they will. In the spirit of full disclosure, I am a nomad, for I live in Hampton Township, Pennsylvania, but the school where I teach is in Evanston, Illinois, and the 412-mile commute does not strike me as odd or cumbersome, for to a large extent it does not matter where I am to get much of my work done. We can gain some greater clarity on the value of mobility by looking at three nomadic preferences.[8]

First, space is preferred over place. "Space" refers to a physical or virtual locale that is chosen and temporary, whereas "place" is a material location that is given and enduring. To illustrate the difference, late modern nomads spend a lot of time in airports. They are not only staging areas for travelers, but also beehives of feverish activity. There are swarms of people rushing to and from gates, and a din of conversations pervades nearly every corner. But few are interacting with anyone in the building. Most are on their smartphones or tablets either talking, emailing, texting, tweeting, surfing, reading, writing, or listening to music. They are busy creating their private spaces in a shared place where they would prefer not to be.

Technologies are employed that effectively erect borders to maintain spaces that are not predicated upon either shared locale or time. Those in

---

8. The following descriptions of these preferences are adapted from Brent Waters, *Christian Moral Theology in the Emerging Technoculture: From Posthuman Back to Human* (Burlington: Ashgate, 2014).

close proximity are not admitted to these protected spaces because they are not needed or relevant. The resulting indifference or even rudeness, however, is not the principal issue at stake. There is nothing inherently wrong with creating such spaces when privacy is required. Indeed, the advent of handy gadgets aiding the preservation of private space is a welcomed revenge of the introverted against the gregarious.

What is troubling is when it is believed that space is an adequate substitute that can entirely supersede place. Our identities are formed in relationships and communities comprised of people both of and not of our choosing. Spaces tend to exclude while places tend to include. Moreover, one needs to be in place for formative relationships to endure and flourish over time, something that a strong desire for speed and mobility do not promote. Posting on Facebook, for instance, is not the same thing as a face-to-face conversation. What happens to a sense of self and others when we increasingly see all interactions as nothing but a series of temporary interactions?

The reader may object that my unease is misplaced. Late modern nomads know the difference between the real and the virtual, despite their privileging of space over place and the corresponding fascination with technology that makes this possible. Yet as Sherry Turkle contends: "Technology proposes itself as the architect of our intimacies. These days, it suggests substitutions that put the real on the run."[9] Increasingly, more people are becoming at home with a fabricated world and are happy with the illusion of intimacy it provides, and the ease with which technology can mask loneliness. Virtual companions are more reliable and less likely to disappoint, because they provide "relationships the way we want them."[10]

To simply reassure ourselves that we need not worry because we know the difference between the virtual and real is naïve, for as Turkle states, "Gradually, we come to see our online life as life itself."[11] In the novel *All the Sad Young Literary Men*,[12] there is a poignant moment when a young, promising author believes that both his work and life are shrinking, because his Google searches of himself produce fewer and fewer hits. If he

---

9. Sherry Turkle, *Alone Together: Why We Expect More from Technology and Less from Each Other* (New York: Basic Books, 2011), 1.

10. Turkle, *Alone Together*, 12.

11. Turkle, *Alone Together*, 17.

12. Keith Gessen, *All the Sad Young Literary Men* (New York: Viking, 2008), 79–81.

disappears altogether from Google, he worries, will he cease, for all practical purposes, to exist?

Second, information is preferred over narration. Late modern nomads want to know a little about a lot of things, and they want to know it quickly. Information is useful in creating those temporary spaces in which fluid identities are formed and expressed. What is not needed or wanted are long and complicated stories that require a lot of time to understand and contemplate. Unlike information, good narration does not lend itself to being easily manipulated, but pulls the reader or listener into its domain, often prompting unanticipated moments of prolonged thinking and deliberation.

Information is admittedly useful; better to be informed than not is a good rule. But information cannot do the work that only narration can do. We are, both implicitly and explicitly, story-formed people; we are shaped by the stories we read, and those we tell. And a story is not just conveying or receiving information. Rather, a compelling story requires its acceptance as such, prompting corresponding changes in one's outlook and actions. The gospel, for example, is not simply a compilation of religious information, but a story that captures and transforms a person's being and doing.

Following Arendt again,[13] knowing and thinking are not synonymous. Knowledge of certain facts and skills enables one to accomplish certain tasks. For example, you need to know how to write to be a writer. In this respect, Bacon was right; knowledge is power. But knowledge alone does not lead to meaning. This requires sustained and disciplined thinking about important but complex ideas and arguments, a wrestling with narration rather than a mastery of information. Simply knowing how to write does not guarantee that an author will write anything worth reading. More importantly, Arendt worried that in the absence of thinking, a person's conscience remains underdeveloped as witnessed by the banality of Adolf Eichmann.[14]

This difference between knowing and thinking, between information and narration, has some important educational implications. To oversimplify: is the primary purpose of a school to give (sell?) its students knowledge, or to help them think? The two are not unrelated, but increasingly we are emphasizing knowledge and information given the demands of a

---

13. See Arendt, *The Life of the Mind*.

14. See Hannah Arendt, *Eichmann in Jerusalem: A Report on the Banality of Evil* (New York: Penguin, 1992).

nomadic society. This tension is being felt at the seminary where I teach. There are some things that all students preparing for the ministry need to know, such as how to prepare a sermon or which end of the baby to baptize. But I am encountering students who want to know some information about such key doctrines as Christology and eschatology (at least enough to pass the ordination exams) but are not too keen on thinking through what these doctrines might mean for their lives and ministries. I fear that over time ministry may be reduced to performance rather than a pastoral relationship that helps people to enter a deeper and fuller relationship with Christ. In short, we need informed knowledge, but it is not enough. We also require thoughtful narration.

Third, exchange is preferred over communication.[15] Exchange is a basic and common human activity. I give you something, and you give me something in return. Without exchange our lives would be deeply impoverished, because it is virtually impossible to live a life of complete self-sufficiency. This is why modern economies are based on the specialization of labor in order to produce a vast range of goods and services that can be exchanged. In contrast, communication is derived from the Greek word *koinonia*. It can be translated variously as "community," "communion," or "communicate." Unlike an exchange in which what is yours becomes mine, and mine becomes yours, what is yours and mine becomes ours. To communicate means sharing certain goods that bind a people together.

To reiterate, exchange is important, and various technologies both enable and enlarge opportunities for exchange on a global scale. It is easy to see why exchange is a key feature of the emerging technoculture, for its nomadic inhabitants require easy access to information, goods, and services that can be produced and consumed quickly, and preferably anytime and anywhere. But the technologies enabling such rapid and easy exchange are also rendering the parties to these exchanges increasingly invisible.

To illustrate, let us imagine that I need a new laptop computer so I can continue to write books and articles that are read by very few people. While on a trip in a hotel room late at night I order the laptop of my dreams online, and request delivery on the day that I will return home. In the few minutes that it took me to complete this task, I initiated a series of global transactions. Although the lead office of the company from which I purchased the

---

15. The following contrast between exchange and communication is adapted from Brent Waters, *Just Capitalism: A Christian Ethic of Economic Globalization* (Louisville: Westminster John Knox, 2016).

computer is in California, the server hosting the website is in Vancouver. An office worker in Dublin reviews and processes my order. The hardware and software were manufactured in such places as Bucharest, Seattle, Seoul, and Taipei. My dream computer is assembled in Shanghai, and airfreighted and delivered to my door at the time promised by a corporation headquartered in Memphis.

What I want to emphasize in this scenario is the range of exchanges that I participated in, involving many different people at the various stages of manufacturing, sales, and delivery, cutting across various geographic locations, time zones, national and jurisdictional borders. Presumably, all the parties benefited from these exchanges: I got my computer, workers received wages, and corporations generated a profit. Yet the entire process is anonymous: I don't anticipate ever meeting anyone who participated in these exchanges. Moreover, within the emerging technoculture, the parties to an exchange are rendered effectively invisible. When I click "purchase this item," rarely if ever do I have in mind all the people required to obtain my wanted item. Don't get me wrong, I am not opposed to anonymous exchange. I don't think my life would be enriched if I had lengthy conversations with every banker, merchant, and sales representative that I do business with. All I want to do is bring to our attention that increasingly anonymous and invisible exchanges have their costs and limits.

At the most basic level it needs to be recognized that exchange taking place in a physical marketplace is different than the exchange occurring in an amorphous global market-space. A trivial example: one day I went to the barbershop and after getting my haircut realized I didn't have any cash and my barber does not accept credit cards. I suggested that I go to the bank to get some money, and offered my mobile phone as a hostage to ensure my payment. She rejected my offer and told me to pay her the next time I was in the area. I doubt if a similar arrangement would ever occur on any commercial website.

Although too much should not be read into this example, it nevertheless reveals an important element underpinning exchange, namely, familiarity and trust. Over the years my barber and I have become familiar to each other and she trusts that I will pay her for a haircut as I have always done in the past. On that embarrassing day, she assumed that my empty wallet was the result of my absentmindedness (I am, after all, a professor) and not a ploy to deceive her. But more broadly, we run into each other occasionally at the grocery store or some public event, and we chat about topics other than haircuts. There is a sense that we share, however vaguely and tenuously, a larger association that, although supported by commercial activities, is not entirely predicated upon or determined by exchanges. In short, we communicate, at least a little bit.

More importantly, it also needs to be recognized that in some instances exchange is not a fitting act at all, and can prove to be a distraction or worse. Parents, for instance, should not bill their children for the care they provide. Rather, as a family they communicate shared goods over time. Exchange is necessary and good, but it cannot buy the good life.

What challenges does this emerging technoculture present for acts of confession, repentance, and forgiveness? At the most basic level, it lessens or eliminates any need to confess, repent, or forgive. Given the preferences for space, information, and exchange, this is not surprising. More often than not, forgiveness, predicated on prior confession and repentance, seeks to mend frayed or broken bonds of enduring human relationships. This is why it is a costly process, because it presupposes bonds of imperfection, shared among people over time. For late modern nomads, these bonds are at best weak, and at worse impediments best discarded to enhance mobility. To be constantly on the move, one cannot be constricted by bonds requiring frequent attention and repair.

To illustrate, Maggie Jackson records the reply of a business executive when asked if it is difficult to become rooted in Canton (a suburb of New York) where she has recently relocated: "'I don't have any interest in being rooted here, honestly,' she said slowly. 'My safety net is made up of individuals. So while I need to have associations with time and space, I can be anywhere.' And she laughed."[16] Another quote from a "global nomad" (Fleura Bardhi): "'It's important for me to establish a quick sense of home. You can leave the next day and not miss your neighbors,' says Bardhi. 'I can't allow myself to fully be comfortable, feel at home and identify with a place.'"[17]

There is little, if any, sense of belonging to a place, and thereby the people associated with it. To be liberated from the constraints of belonging somewhere and with others means, ideally, nomads have no past or future, only perpetually becoming what they will, and they aspire to become free-floating global souls. Consequently, except in cases involving willful

---

16. Maggie Jackson, *Distracted: The Erosion of Attention and the Coming Dark Age* (Amherst: Prometheus, 2008), 99.

17. Jackson, *Distracted*, 112–13.

violence, fraud, and the like, harming another global soul bumped into is usually perceived as an excusable mistake; nothing of any lasting importance requiring the difficult work of confessing, repenting, and forgiving. All that is needed is a diffident recognition of a casual apology. (An aside: I don't know the extent to which nomadic global souls populate the church, but I fear it is extensive, at least judging by the Protestant circles that I frequent in which generic prayers of confession sound increasingly like variations on the phrase, "Oops, I did it again.")

At a deeper level, however, confession, repentance, and forgiveness are problematic in the emerging technoculture because its nomadic inhabitants lack proper self-understanding, and therefore a disordered self-love. Indeed, there may be few genuine selves wandering about. This is counterintuitive given the premium placed upon the individual assertive will, so let me explain. Borrowing the words of Ellen Charry: "To know God is to know ourselves, and understanding ourselves theocentrically in terms of Genesis 1:26 is true self-knowledge for true self-love. True self-love is the healing of disordered love (i.e., sin)."[18] And only the "healed person can love well, and loving well is the basis of a flourishing life."[19] A flourishing life is synonymous with being happy, and a "happy life is not sensational" because it does not "mistake excitement for happiness."[20] Moreover, a properly ordered self-love upon which flourishing or happiness is based cannot be constructed but only embraced. To add to Charry's work, it is within a properly ordered love of God, self, and neighbors that frequent confession, repentance, and forgiveness are needed to learn how to love well.

This scheme, however, is nearly unintelligible to the nomadic wanderers of the emerging technoculture, for the self itself is an artifact of the will. And these artifacts are constantly being constructed and reconstructed within temporary spaces that in turn are also being constructed and reconstructed. Ideally there are no enduring selves, only free-floating souls adapting to rapidly changing circumstances that occasionally collide with other free-floating souls. Or in Jackson's chilling words: "We are ghosts moving in and out of each other's consciousness, often silently but sometimes with a shriek and a howl."[21] Unlike the title of Charry's book,

---

18. Ellen T. Charry, *God and the Art of Happiness* (Grand Rapids: Eerdmans, 2010) 157.

19. Ibid., 159.

20. Ibid., 219–20.

21. Jackson, *Distracted*, 58.

there is no art of happiness to be learned, only techniques for achieving temporary, sequential, and ever more exciting pleasures to be mastered. In the unremitting flux of the emerging technoculture in which any sense of relative permanence should be eschewed, there is simply no need or use for confession, repentance, and forgiveness, for how free-floating souls or ghosts really harm or sin against each other.

Although the notion of sin has fallen into disfavor in the emerging technoculture, its residue continues to exert a largely unrecognized but widespread public influence, and we especially enjoy exposing the sins committed by others. How else to explain the accusatory rhetoric that now passes for political discourse? But I digress.

For nearly two millennia, moral theologians have spilled a lot of ink defining and categorizing sin. But for the purposes of this chapter two types will do, namely, sins of commission and sins of omission. The former are willful acts that harm our neighbors or ourselves, whereas the latter are acts we fail to do. In both instances, we can sin against God either through willful defiance or failing to do what is required of us. Historically, more attention has been devoted to sins of commission than omission. This is understandable since sin can only be understood in relation to forgiveness, and only those acts that should be punished can be forgiven. It is more clear-cut to assign blame and punishment to acts that are committed than failing to act. If I pick your pocket, for example, I am clearly culpable and deserve punishment, whereas if I didn't try to prevent someone from picking your pocket it is not so clear that I have done anything punishable, though I failed you as a neighbor.

I fear that in a culture increasingly dedicated to asserting greater mastery over nature and human nature, sins of omission are becoming center place. Individuals will effectively be held culpable or stigmatized by failing to assert greater mastery over their lives and circumstances when it is within their power to do so. We are already seeing subtle signs of this shift. Why are those overweight people failing to take care of themselves through proper diets and exercise? Or why is the mastery of basic computer skills a prerequisite of college admission when it is not clear that individuals unable or unwilling to surf the web are any less intelligent? I don't think it is far-fetched to worry that increasingly people will be judged to be irresponsible, or worse, for failing to take advantage of technological interventions and applications at their disposal. To return to the previous instances of issues at the beginning and end of life that I mentioned: Why did *you* allow the birth of a child with severe disabilities when *you* could have prevented it? Why are *you* failing to accept the offer of an assisted easy death since the quality of your life is so obviously diminished? Increasingly, the onus will be placed on people to justify their failures to act, and I suspect they will not be easily forgiven, if at all.

Why do I find this troubling? At least by concentrating on sins of commission there is always the possibility of restored fellowship with God and neighbor. The prospect of forgiveness and absolution is an outcome of attempting to right the wrong committed following confession, repentance, and amendment of life. But how do I right a wrong resulting from my failure to act? If failing to prevent the birth of a defective child or using assisted dying are "sins," how can I ever be forgiven or absolved since the wrong can never be righted. Even more troubling, identifying and punishing sins of omission have always been useful tools of tyranny. The tyrant routinely punishes those who fail to conform to expected patterns of behavior and conduct; the tyrant can punish those failing to identify the misdeeds of their neighbors; the tyrant can even punish those failing to think correctly. Tyranny flourishes when people mistrust and fear one another. To be clear, I am *not* suggesting that the emerging technoculture will end inevitably in tyranny. But I do fear that in asserting ever greater technological mastery we may produce a people who are less trusting and forgiving, and that is not a strategy for promoting human flourishing.

If you and I live in a culture with a strong proclivity to discount or dismiss the need for confession, repentance, and forgiveness, then we also live in a culture that is not predisposed for healing its disordered loves. As Christians, what should we then do? There are two bad options. First, there is the Borg option of embracing the culture fully since resistance is futile. We should adapt our belief in sin as something excusable and act accordingly. This also means that desire cannot be healed, and we will not learn to love well. This option effectively renders the world, God's creation, as irredeemable.

The second bad option is a sectarian-Luddite refusal of the culture. As Christians, we should, as much as possible, inoculate ourselves from the contamination of the surrounding culture, withdrawing into physical or spiritual enclaves where we may practice a purer faith. This option, however, is itself a disordered love, for it effectively rejects the world as God's good creation. That which God loves is made unlovable and unworthy of healing.

Repentance and Forgiveness

A preferable option is one of engaging and selectively resisting the culture. In engaging the culture, it must be kept in mind that we are not encountering wicked people, but predominantly people loving good things badly. Presumably it should be easy for Christians to engage their nomadic neighbors, for they share many things in common. Christians are a mobile people. Christianity has never been a territorial religion. The church exists wherever two or three are gathered in the name of Jesus Christ. In serving their Lord, Christians are always on the move, going wherever in the world God calls them to be, for however short or lengthy period of time is needed, and the speed of their journeys may sometimes be slow and sometimes fast.

Yet there is an important difference. Christians are not nomads; they are pilgrims; their life is one of perpetual pilgrimage. Using Saint Augustine's imagery of the two cities, Christians are citizens of the heavenly city, but they presently reside in the earthly city. Consequently, they are never entirely at home anywhere in the world and are always a bit restless anticipating their final destination of eternal fellowship with God. Christians should invite their nomadic neighbors to become pilgrims, because it is a better life. This invitation, however, requires that Christians order their lives in ways that demonstrate why their life of pilgrimage is in fact better, and in doing so bear witness to their Lord within the earthly city, and to love and serve their neighbors in Christ's name. And to love them properly, they must be a habitually confessing, repenting, and forgiving people; this is our witness.

How are such habits formed? Pilgrims know that they must at times stop and be in place; whenever two or three gather, they gather somewhere. In their gathering, they hear again and are formed by the gospel: God's story of good news. In their gathering, they communicate the goods of God's creation; they love the world created and redeemed by God. In this place, in this narrative, and in this communication, disordered love is healed in a habitually confessing, repenting, and forgiving people. Such habituation is difficult and costly. To illustrate this difficulty and cost, I turn to Anne Tyler's novel *Saint Maybe*.[22]

Ian Bedloe is a college student. His older brother, Danny, marries Lucy. Lucy has two young children from a previous marriage, and becomes pregnant a bit too early after the wedding. After the birth of the baby, Ian

---

22. Anne Tyler, *Saint Maybe* (New York: Ivy, 1991). The following is taken, with slight alterations, from Brent Waters, "Worship and the Shape of the Christian Moral Life," *Doxology* 27 (2010) 30–33.

becomes Lucy's preferred babysitter. He notices that her behavior is erratic, even suspicious. She is gone for long periods of time and cannot give a credible explanation of what she has been doing, and she often returns home with clothes or other items she obviously cannot afford. Ian suspects that she is having an affair. One evening, Lucy returns home late, ruining Ian's plans for a romantic rendezvous with his girlfriend. He is angry and confronts his brother, accusing Lucy of infidelity and suggesting that the baby is not his. Danny is devastated, and a bit later, without talking to Lucy, he commits suicide. A few months later Lucy, either mistakenly or intentionally, takes an overdose of sleeping pills and dies as well, leaving three orphaned children.

Ian grows increasingly troubled about his complicity in this tragic set of circumstances. One night while walking along some downtown street he sees a storefront lit up and stumbles into the Church of the Second Chance. Having grown up in a mainline Protestant church, he finds the service to be rather odd. There is no apparent structure, the so-called hymns are syrupy, and at one point individuals offer random prayer requests ranging from the mundane to the bizarre. Much to his surprise, Ian blurts out: "Pray for me to be good again. Pray for me to be forgiven."[23]

After the service, the minister, Reverend Emmett, asks Ian if his prayer request had been answered, to which he replies, "Not exactly." Reverend Emmett then asks, "What was it that you needed forgiven?"

Ian couldn't believe his ears. Was this even legal, inquiring into a person's private prayers? He ought to spin on his heel and walk out. But instead his heart began hammering as if he were about to do something brave. In a voice not quite his own, he said, "I caused my brother to, um, kill himself."

Reverend Emmett gazed at him thoughtfully.

"I told him his wife was cheating on him," Ian said in a rush, "and now I'm not even sure she was. So he drove into a wall. And then his wife died of sleeping pills and I guess you could say I caused that too, more or less . . ."[24] He goes on to explain about the children. After an awkward silence, Ian asks, "Don't you think I'm forgiven?"

"Goodness no," Reverend Emmett said briskly.

Ian's mouth fell open. He wondered if he'd misunderstood. He said, "I'm *not* forgiven?"

"Oh, no."

---

23. Tyler, *Saint Maybe*, 129.
24. Tyler, *Saint Maybe*, 132.

Repentance and Forgiveness

"But . . . I thought that was kind of the point," Ian said. "I thought God forgives everything."

"He does," Reverend Emmett said. "But you can't just say, 'I'm sorry God.' Why anyone could do that much! You have to offer reparation—concrete, practical reparation."

"But what if there isn't any reparation? What if it's something nothing will fix?"

"Well, that's where Jesus comes in, of course."

Another itchy word: Jesus. Ian averted his eyes.

"Jesus remembers how difficult life on earth can be," Reverend Emmett told him. "He helps with what you can't undo. But only after you've *tried* to undo it."

"Tried? Tried how?" Ian asked. "What would it take?"[25]

After another awkward silence, Reverend Emmett replies, "Well, first you'll need to see to those children."

"Okay. But . . . see to them in what way, exactly?"

"Why raise them, I suppose."

"Huh?" Ian said. "But I'm only a freshman!"

"Then maybe you should drop out."

"Drop out?"

"Right."

"Drop out of college?"

"Right."[26]

Ian goes on to complain how crazy this is. It would destroy his plans and ruin his parents' dreams about his future. He offers one final protest: "I can't take on a bunch of kids! Who do you think I am? I'm nineteen years old!" Ian said. "What kind of a cockeyed religion *is* this?"

"It's the religion of atonement and complete forgiveness," Reverend Emmett said. "It's the religion of the Second Chance."[27]

Ian Bedloe does drop out of college, and the remainder of the story is about his raising the children until they become adults, and the consequent twists and turns his life takes in pursuing this cockeyed religion. We may want to quarrel with Reverend Emmett's doctrinal expositions, and we may find the liturgy of the Church of the Second Chance to be wanting, but all the important elements are in this story. There is confession without

---

25. Tyler, *Saint Maybe*, 133 (emphasis original).
26. Tyler, *Saint Maybe*, 133–34.
27. Tyler, *Saint Maybe*, 134 (emphasis original).

excuse; contrite repentance; amendment of life and presumably forgiveness in the end. *Saint Maybe* is a story of healing disordered love, a difficult and costly story, but one that needs to be told, in word and deed, in the emerging technoculture.

www.ingramcontent.com/pod-product-compliance
Lightning Source LLC
Chambersburg PA
CBHW032236080426
42735CB00008B/882